Image Processing with

Second Edition

Extract and analyze data from complex images with ImageJ, the world's leading image processing tool

Jurjen Broeke

José María Mateos Pérez

Javier Pascau

BIRMINGHAM - MUMBAI

Image Processing with ImageJ
Second Edition

First published: September 2013

Second edition: November 2015

Production reference: 1241115

Published by Packt Publishing Ltd.
Livery Place
35 Livery Street
Birmingham B3 2PB, UK.

ISBN 978-1-78588-983-7

www.packtpub.com

Credits

Authors
Jurjen Broeke
José María Mateos Pérez
Javier Pascau

Reviewer
Jan Eglinger

Commissioning Editor
Neil Alexander

Acquisition Editor
Manish Nainani

Content Development Editor
Sumeet Sawant

Technical Editor
Parag Topre

Copy Editor
Karuna Narayanan

Project Coordinator
Shweta H Birwatkar

Proofreader
Safis Editing

Indexer
Monica Ajmera Mehta

Graphics
Disha Haria

Production Coordinator
Conidon Miranda

Cover Work
Conidon Miranda

About the Authors

Jurjen Broeke has a PhD in neuroscience from Vrije Universiteit (VU) Amsterdam and uses live-cell imaging techniques to study the fundamental processes of neuronal function. As a neuroscientist, he studies the processes involved in neural communication. Besides acquiring images, Jurjen also develops software to analyze dynamics in ImageJ, MATLAB, and R. When not enjoying the outdoors and taking pictures, he develops technical hardware and software solutions in the Department of Functional Genomics at VU.

José María Mateos Pérez is a Spanish postdoctoral fellow at the Montreal Neurological Institute (http://www.mcgill.ca/neuro/), where his main research lines deal with neurodevelopment and machine learning applied to clinical prediction. He has also been an experienced ImageJ user and has developed several macros and plugins. One of them, jClustering, has been published in PLOS ONE, a peer-reviewed journal. When he has enough time to procrastinate, he also likes to develop data analysis tools in Python and R.

Javier Pascau received his PhD from Polytechnic University in Madrid in 2006 and is currently a visiting professor at Carlos III University, Madrid. He has been a part of Biomedical Imaging and Instrumentation Group, a research laboratory with a multidisciplinary team of engineers, physicists, biologists, and physicians located both in the university as well as Hospital General Universitario Gregorio Marañón (biig.uc3m.es). Javier's research and teaching cover areas such as medical image processing, analysis, quantification, and multimodal registration, both in preclinical and clinical environments. He has been involved in the development of small animal PET and CT devices. In the last few years, Javier has led several projects on intraoperative radiation therapy and image-guided surgery. He has authored more than 40 papers published in peer-reviewed journals over the last 15 years.

I want to thank all my colleagues at the university and the hospital, since my knowledge on image processing is the result of multiple interactions in this multidisciplinary environment.

About the Reviewer

Jan Eglinger works as an image processing specialist at Friedrich Miescher Institute for Biomedical Research in Basel, Switzerland. Jan received a master's degree in biotechnology from ESBS in Strasbourg, France, and a PhD in cell biology from MPI-CBG in Dresden, Germany. He has been contributing to Fiji and ImageJ development since 2010.

www.PacktPub.com

Support files, eBooks, discount offers, and more

For support files and downloads related to your book, please visit www.PacktPub.com.

Did you know that Packt offers eBook versions of every book published, with PDF and ePub files available? You can upgrade to the eBook version at www.PacktPub. com and as a print book customer, you are entitled to a discount on the eBook copy. Get in touch with us at service@packtpub.com for more details.

At www.PacktPub.com, you can also read a collection of free technical articles, sign up for a range of free newsletters and receive exclusive discounts and offers on Packt books and eBooks.

https://www2.packtpub.com/books/subscription/packtlib

Do you need instant solutions to your IT questions? PacktLib is Packt's online digital book library. Here, you can search, access, and read Packt's entire library of books.

Why subscribe?

- Fully searchable across every book published by Packt
- Copy and paste, print, and bookmark content
- On demand and accessible via a web browser

Free access for Packt account holders

If you have an account with Packt at www.PacktPub.com, you can use this to access PacktLib today and view 9 entirely free books. Simply use your login credentials for immediate access.

Table of Contents

Preface

Advances in image processing are vital for the science and technology communities. However, as images become larger and more complex, even more advanced processing techniques are required. Automation becomes necessary too so that you can perform simple tasks easily and focus on more sophisticated issues. ImageJ is here to help—as one of the key powerful tools in the development of image processing, it lets you extract even more useful data from your images.

What this book covers

Chapter 1, Getting Started with ImageJ, takes a look at the origin and use of ImageJ and discusses how to download and install it on different platforms. We will also take a look at the basic folder structure of ImageJ installation and configure it to be used.

Chapter 2, Basic Image Processing with ImageJ, discusses the different image types that are supported by ImageJ. You will also learn how to load images from a disk or URL. We will take a look at the anatomy of an image window in ImageJ and the information that can be viewed. It will also deal with image scaling, calibration, lookup tables, adjusting image size, and adjusting channels.

Chapter 3, Advanced Image Processing with ImageJ, investigates the processing of different types of images. We will take a look at different sources of noise that can corrupt images and degrade their quality. You will also learn how to apply different corrections to images to fix these problems.

Chapter 4, Image Segmentation and Feature Extraction with ImageJ, looks at the ways to separate an image into a foreground and background. We will consider different methods to set the threshold in grayscale and color images.

Chapter 5, Basic Measurements with ImageJ, considers some methods to measure the parameters within images and time series. We will apply some of the techniques discussed in previous chapters to extract data from our images. You will also learn how to visualize dynamic data in a single image (kymographs).

Chapter 6, Developing Macros in ImageJ, discusses how to create a macro using a recorder to discover the commands and functions that we can apply. Next, we will take a look at processing a folder full of images and saving the resulting images to the hard disk. Finally, we will look at the Batch Process mode, which allows ImageJ to process a folder in a similar way.

Chapter 7, Explanation of ImageJ Constructs, looks at the framework of macros and plugins that are available in ImageJ. We will discuss some of the constructs that the ImageJ API exposes for use in scripting and plugins. Finally, we will describe how to set up an IDE to develop ImageJ and plugins using it as a standalone or Maven-based project.

Chapter 8, Anatomy of ImageJ Plugins, takes a look at the anatomy of plugins for ImageJ1.x and ImageJ2. We will also take a look at some of the specific constructs that are used in plugins for both frameworks. This chapter examines how to compile, run, and debug plugins using the IDE or tools provided by ImageJ.

Chapter 9, Creating ImageJ Plugins for Analysis, develops a plugin from scratch using the Maven system and NetBeans IDE. We will discuss how to add a basic user interface to our plugin, allowing the user to change some of the parameters that influence the way the plugin functions. We will also add an external library to provide additional functionality that was not present in ImageJ.

Chapter 10, Where to Go from Here, sums up the topics that are discussed in previous chapters and provides further resources that are available for you to continue developing your own plugins. The chapter also looks at some of the more advanced techniques that are available for developers.

What you need for this book

You'll need the following software for the book:

ImageJ 1.4x or Fiji

- NetBeans 8.0.2+

Who this book is for

This book is created for engineers, scientists, and developers eager to tackle image processing with one of the leading tools in the field for image processing and analysis. No prior knowledge of ImageJ is needed. Familiarity with Java programming will be needed for readers to code their own routines using ImageJ.

Conventions

In this book, you will find a number of styles of text that distinguish between different kinds of information. Here are some examples of these styles, and an explanation of their meaning.

Code words in text, database table names, folder names, filenames, file extensions, pathnames, dummy URLs, user input, and Twitter handles are shown as follows: "The two most important folders are the macros and plugins folders."

A block of code is set as follows:

```
varmyTools = newMenu("My awesome tools",
newArray("Macro_1", "Macro_2", "-", "Macro_3"));

macro"My awesome tools - C037T0b11MT7b09aTcb09t" {
  cmd = getArgument();
  if(cmd== "Macro_1")
  runMacro("/PATH/TO/Macro_1_tool");
  else if(cmd == "Macro_2)"
  runMacro("/PATH/TO/some_other_tool");
}
```

New terms and **important words** are shown in bold. Words that you see on the screen, in menus or dialog boxes for example, appear in the text like this: "We can now perform the particle analysis by selecting **Analyze | Analyze Particles...** from the menu."

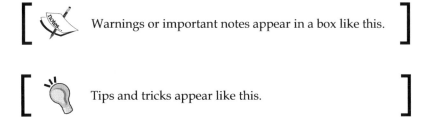

Warnings or important notes appear in a box like this.

Tips and tricks appear like this.

Reader feedback

Feedback from our readers is always welcome. Let us know what you think about this book—what you liked or may have disliked. Reader feedback is important for us to develop titles that you really get the most out of.

To send us general feedback, simply send an e-mail to feedback@packtpub.com, and mention the book title via the subject of your message.

If there is a topic that you have expertise in and you are interested in either writing or contributing to a book, see our author guide on www.packtpub.com/authors.

Customer support

Now that you are the proud owner of a Packt book, we have a number of things to help you to get the most from your purchase.

Downloading the example code

You can download the example code files for all Packt books you have purchased from your account at http://www.packtpub.com. If you purchased this book elsewhere, you can visit http://www.packtpub.com/support and register to have the files e-mailed directly to you.

Errata

Although we have taken every care to ensure the accuracy of our content, mistakes do happen. If you find a mistake in one of our books—maybe a mistake in the text or the code—we would be grateful if you would report this to us. By doing so, you can save other readers from frustration and help us improve subsequent versions of this book. If you find any errata, please report them by visiting http://www.packtpub.com/submit-errata, selecting your book, clicking on the **errata submission form** link, and entering the details of your errata. Once your errata are verified, your submission will be accepted and the errata will be uploaded on our website, or added to any list of existing errata, under the Errata section of that title. Any existing errata can be viewed by selecting your title from http://www.packtpub.com/support.

Piracy

Piracy of copyright material on the Internet is an ongoing problem across all media. At Packt, we take the protection of our copyright and licenses very seriously. If you come across any illegal copies of our works, in any form, on the Internet, please provide us with the location address or website name immediately so that we can pursue a remedy.

Please contact us at copyright@packtpub.com with a link to the suspected pirated material.

We appreciate your help in protecting our authors, and our ability to bring you valuable content.

Questions

You can contact us at questions@packtpub.com if you are having a problem with any aspect of the book, and we will do our best to address it.

1
Getting Started with ImageJ

Welcome to the second edition of *Image Processing with ImageJ*. ImageJ is a versatile and open source software package designed for scientific image processing and analysis. It is written in the Java programming language, allowing for a uniform cross-platform experience. It is based on the NIH Image software package on the Macintosh platform, developed in 1987 by Wayne Rasband. Rasband, who is still an active contributor of ImageJ, published the first ImageJ distribution in 1997. It was developed as a project to provide a solution to a problem. In 2012, ImageJ celebrated its twenty-fifth birthday with a publication in the journal Nature Methods.

ImageJ distributions

Currently, there are different distributions that are based on or are extensions of the original ImageJ. The basic ImageJ package is available on the ImageJ website at the National Institute of Health (`http://imagej.nih.gov/ij/download.html`). The current version of the package is **version 1.50b**, and the website is updated monthly. This is the core distribution of ImageJ, which contains the main interface and all the basic tools to load, view, process, and export images and data. Other distributions contain this core package and most of its features, but you need to add additional features and plugins to create an optimized interface for specific fields. Some of these other distributions are still easily recognizable as ImageJ, while others offer a completely different interface.

For different scientific fields, different distributions were developed based on the core of ImageJ. One of the major distributions for the life sciences is called **Fiji** (Fiji Is Just ImageJ), which can be found on the Fiji website (http://fiji.sc/Fiji). The basis of Fiji is ImageJ, but it comes with a large complement of preinstalled features (macros and plugins) that are commonly used for image processing in the life sciences. It is focused on fluorescence microscopy, with built-in tools for segmentation, visualization, and co-localization. It also contains plugins for image registration, particle tracking, and super-resolution processing and reconstruction. It also has an extensive library of image formats that can be opened. This library includes proprietary image formats from all the major acquisition software packages via the **Bio-Formats** plugin, as described in the upcoming section. The advantages of this distribution are the large number of supplied plugins that come with it as well as a very user-friendly script editor. It also has an extensive update mechanism for both ImageJ as well as some plugins.

For the field of astronomy, a different distribution of ImageJ was developed, named **AstroImageJ** (http://www.astro.louisville.edu/software/astroimagej/). This distribution takes the core implementation of ImageJ and supplements it with specific plugins and macros developed for analysis in the field of astronomy. It is not directly compatible with ImageJ. The core of ImageJ was slightly modified for this distribution.

An example of a distribution derived from ImageJ but with a different user interface is **Icy** (http://icy.bioimageanalysis.org/). The Icy distribution has integrated ImageJ, and many plugins are compatible. However, not every plugin developed for ImageJ will work within Icy and vice versa. In the Icy distribution, there is a strong emphasis on cellular and spot detection and tracking. There is also a strong emphasis on plugin development. Plugins that are developed for the Icy platform will have documentation and automated updating implemented by design. There are also possibilities for users to directly provide feedback to the developers from within the interface, which is a feature not present within other distributions based on ImageJ. A disadvantage may be that it requires several external libraries to be installed, most importantly VTK, which can cause issues on Linux systems.

Another distribution that uses ImageJ not only for the processing of data but also aids in the acquisition of data is called **µManager**, which can be found at https://www.micro-manager.org/. It is loaded from within ImageJ as a plugin, but provides a unique interface geared towards image acquisition and hardware control. Camera and microscope drivers allow the control of supported hardware used in image acquisition, which can then be fed directly to ImageJ for processing and analysis. An example of the use of µManager is in the Open SPIM project, where it is used to control a DIY light sheet microscope, acquire images, and process them.

The uses of ImageJ

ImageJ is a great tool to process images and perform analysis. It is used in many scientific peer-reviewed publications, with over 1000 articles in diverse fields such as life sciences, astronomy, and physics. In life sciences, it is used to quantify medical images to aid in the detection of pathological markers. It is also used to process and quantify data from single-cell or single-molecule experiments using super-resolution techniques such as **STORM** and **PALM**. In physics and engineering, it is used to quantify and visualize data obtained from atomic force microscopy. For astronomy, ImageJ is used to analyze images obtained from telescopes and satellites and visualize data obtained from observatories. NASA's Jet Propulsion Laboratory hosts a central node with a good collection of data that is available for download at `http://pds.jpl.nasa.gov/`. It contains information on the planetary missions as well as other research fields such as atmospheres or asteroids.

As it supports a large number of different image formats, it is a great image viewer and allows a great number of pixel-based operations. It also supports images with bit depths greater than 8 or 16 bits per channel. However, it is not meant for anything other than pixel-based operations. If you wish to use vector-based operations, then ImageJ is not the tool for you (unless you wish to develop this functionality).

Besides the common tools for image processing, such as cropping, rotating, and scaling, it supports images with multiple dimensions. Images with up to five dimensions can be processed and saved. These dimensions can include channels (multiple colors), frames (time points), and slices (Z planes), and any combination of these dimensions. Currently, multipoint acquisitions are not supported (different locations in a larger *XY* space). It is also possible to change the intensity of pixels displayed by adjusting the brightness and contrast, or the color-coding of the pixels (**Lookup Tables**). More advanced techniques to correct image acquisition artifacts, such as background and bleaching, are also available.

The default image format of ImageJ is the **Tagged Image File Format** (**TIFF**). This format allows for the storage of multidimensional data and supports many meta-information fields for calibration, data acquisition information, and descriptions. It can also store information about elements such as overlays. Graphical annotations are placed on the image in a separate layer. Measurements will benefit from the calibration included in the image, allowing for a fast feedback of sizes in the appropriate unit. It is, however, less suited for different kinds of mixed data such as video files. Using the **FFMPEG** plugin allows you to open and save the image data of a video but not the audio track(s). Also, editing is limited to a small set of transitions and layering techniques. For editing videos with image and sound, non-linear editors are available. They allow for greater control.

It can also be used as an image-conversion tool. Many image formats can be read natively by ImageJ, and with the help of a plugin, many proprietary formats can be opened. Once the image is opened, it can be saved to any of the supported export formats supported by ImageJ, including, but not limited to TIF, JPG, and PNG for images and AVI and MOV for **time series** and **Z-stacks**. It can also be used to change the order and/or color of images exported by other software. It is, however, not meant as a general photo editor or nonlinear video editor, as it lacks some of the specialized tools required for these workflows.

The current state of ImageJ

Currently, ImageJ has been cited in more than 200 publications since the beginning of 2015, in fields ranging from physics and engineering to medicine and biology. Many publications are about newly developed plugins that were specifically developed to solve a problem within a certain subfield of science. On the ImageJ website, the page that lists plugins has more than 1000 plugins available. A few research institutes even have collections of multiple plugins available that were developed there as research projects. Most, if not all, are open source plugins with the full source code available. You can adjust and customize the code to suit your needs.

ImageJ2

ImageJ is still under active development, and new features and bug fixes are added to the core distribution on a regular basis. Currently, the development of a revised system for ImageJ is being developed. It is called **ImageJ2**. The goals of ImageJ2 are to better support multidimensional data as well as create a more extensible platform that can be used as a library instead of a standalone application. It will also create a more consistent environment for development and extension. One of the features being developed is the updating mechanism for ImageJ. Currently, it is possible to update ImageJ automatically using a central repository, and one of the goals of ImageJ2 is to expand this option to plugins and other features and allow tracking of bugs and features. However, one of the core requirements in the new ImageJ2 system is backward compatibility. This goal means that plugins developed now will stay functional in future releases of ImageJ. The current status is indicated as **beta**, which means the plugin is functional but may still contain bugs and is not optimized for performance yet.

SciFIO and OME-XML

Other developments related to image are those related to image formats and standards. Currently, all major commercial acquisition platforms store image data in unique proprietary file formats. The SCIFIO project is aimed at creating an extensible and integrated interface to handle images of different formats. It will support more image formats and allow for additional options to be set when importing the data, such as autoscaling, loading metadata, and loading the data in different ImageJ image types. However, it is still under active development, and some of the features do not quite work in a production environment (yet).

The **OME-XML (Open Microscopy Environment-XML)** project is aimed at creating a file format that contains all the image and metadata in a standardized format. This would facilitate the exchange of microscope image data, regardless of the equipment used for acquisition. It is mainly focused on the exchange of microscopy data in the field of life sciences. It contains all the experimental and setup data as well as the pixel data in a single file specification.

Bio-formats

Besides the OME-XML format, which is focused on integrating acquisition and processing across multiple acquisition platforms, there is also active development of the plugin used to import many image formats currently in existence. This plugin, called Bio-Formats, is mostly focused on image formats from the life sciences. However, it also supports **FITS** data, which is used in the field of astronomy and space exploration. It currently supports (to different degrees) 140 different image formats and converts them to the OME-XML format for use in ImageJ.

Integrated environment for acquisition and processing

As ImageJ is such an extensible application for acquisition, processing, and analysis, it is impossible to deal with all the options and extensions. In this edition, I will focus on image processing and analysis. I recommend the Fiji distribution for people beginning with ImageJ, as it contains a large number of useful features that allow you to get off to a running start. Another advantage is the presence of the script editor supplied with Fiji, which has many features that some of the larger Java development suites also provide. These features mainly include syntax highlighting and smart indenting. The editor also includes a selection of macro and plugin templates that allow for a basic framework to start with.

Obtaining and installing ImageJ

The current version of ImageJ can be run on any platform that supports Java. When you wish to use ImageJ or one of the other distributions, a version can be downloaded for your specific operating system. A distribution of ImageJ can be downloaded with the **Java Runtime Environment** (**JRE**) prepackaged. The following sections will explain how to obtain and install ImageJ on the three main operating systems: Windows, OS X, and Linux.

Installation of ImageJ

When you download a copy of ImageJ, the JRE can be provided along with it. If you already have a copy of the JRE installed, you could download ImageJ without the JRE for a faster download. The minimal requirements to run ImageJ are JRE Version 1.6 or higher. For some distributions, most notably Fiji, the JRE has to be version 1.6. This limitation is due to the current implementation of the updater included with Fiji, which is not capable of updating the JRE. This problem may be resolved in the future.

As ImageJ comes with its own JRE, it can be extracted on a USB drive and run from there without installation. The only limitations on the system are dependent on the size of the images. ImageJ loads images directly into memory, so the available system memory needs to be large enough to hold the images you wish to process. When memory requirements exceed 3 GB, a 64-bit operating system with a 64-bit JRE is required.

Since ImageJ is platform independent, you could use the same version on all three platforms: Windows, OS X, and Linux. The only platform-dependent part is the JRE; for each platform, there is a specific JRE installation. The following sections will explain how to install ImageJ on each of the operating systems.

Installing on Windows

In order to install ImageJ on Windows, you can download the latest version from the ImageJ website at the **NIH** (`http://imagej.nih.gov/ij/download.html`) or for Fiji from the Fiji website (`http://Fiji.sc/Downloads`). When downloading from the NIH website, there are two choices: an installer for 32-bit or 64-bit systems and a ZIP archive when you wish to run ImageJ on a platform without installer privileges.

When using the installer version, it is generally not recommended that you install ImageJ in the Program Files folder. Certain files within the ImageJ folder need to be modified when using the program, so when running it as a regular user, access problems may occur. Also, when installing or creating plugins, the compiled files nccd to bc placed in the plugins folder within ImageJ. This folder may not have write permission when it is located in the Program Files folder for regular (non-administrator) users. Alternatively, you could change the access permissions for the ImageJ folder specifically. However, this is not recommended from a security point of view.

Double-clicking on the `ImageJ.exe` file within the extracted folder will start ImageJ. This file is a wrapper executable that calls the `ij.jar` file and uses the supplied JRE to run it. The Fiji distribution comes as a ZIP archive that can be extracted on a disk and run immediately:

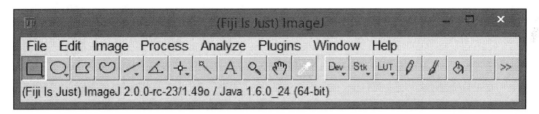

Installing on Mac OS X

ImageJ is available for Mac OS X as a ZIP archive that can be extracted to a folder within the Applications folder. The Fiji distribution can be downloaded as a DMG file that can be dropped in the Applications folder. This will install the ImageJ folder and make it accessible for all registered users. It will also create a Fiji icon in the app drawer. If you wish to import or export QuickTime movies under OS X 10.10 (Yosemite), you need to download the `QTJava.zip` and `libQTJNative.jnilib` files from `http://imagej.nih.gov/ij/download/qt/` into your home directory within the `Library/Java/Extensions` folder.

Note that in OS X 10.7 and later, you may receive a warning the first time you try to run ImageJ. This warning will say **ImageJ can't be opened because it is from an unidentified developer**. This can be resolved by going to the system settings and pushing the allow button in the security and privacy panel. This should prevent this warning from showing up in the future. Alternatively, you can select the Anywhere option from the Allow apps downloaded from section. The latter option is not recommended from a security point of view, as it might also allow malicious software to be executed.

Note that when ImageJ (or Fiji) is run on OS X, the menu bar is not part of the main window as in Windows:

Installing on Linux

ImageJ can be installed on Linux platforms by unpacking the distribution from the NIH website. The distribution from the NIH website is available as a ZIP file, while the Fiji distribution is available as a `tar.gz` file. For most Linux distributions, it is recommended that you extract the archive to a location within your home folder. This prevents problems with write permissions on the ImageJ folders. The folder contains a shell script to run ImageJ. This shell script is named ImageJ. For different desktop environments, methods exist to create a shell shortcut to this script to allow it to run from a shortcut.

The ImageJ folder structure

After installing ImageJ, a folder structure is placed at a location designated during the installation process. This folder's structure consists of a few key folders that are essential to the regular functioning of ImageJ. If you installed ImageJ in a folder to which you have *no write* privileges, there are two important folders that need read and write permissions in order for ImageJ to function: the `plugins` and `macros` folders. Also, the configuration file on Windows platforms (`pref.cfg`) needs write permissions for the user. Without the write permission, settings cannot be changed. The next section briefly explains the properties for the `plugins` and `macros` folders, and how ImageJ uses them.

Plugins folder

The two most important folders are the `macros` and `plugins` folders. These folders will be searched for available macros and plugins when ImageJ loads. When you download a plugin and place it in the `plugins` folder, the plugin will be found the next time ImageJ starts. When downloading plugins, there are three different options of files that can be downloaded: a Java source file (`.java`), a compiled file (`.class`), or a Java archive (`.jar`). In order for plugins to be displayed in the plugins menu, the `.java` and `.class` files need to contain at least one underscore character in the filename. For `.jar` files, the archive needs to contain a `plugins.config` file that defines the location within the menu system. This has an additional advantage that plugins within a `.jar` archive can also be installed outside the plugins `menu`. `Underscores` are replaced by spaces in the plugins menu or removed completely if the last character is an underscore. If you place your plugins in a folder within the `plugins` folder, this folder name will also show up in the **Plugins** menu, but only if it contains at least one valid plugin. If you download the source file of a plugin, you can create an executable plugin by choosing **Compile and Run** from the **Plugins** menu and selecting the Java file. The next time ImageJ is run, the new plugin will be automatically detected.

JAR files are slightly special. They can be placed within the `plugins` folder, but they do not have to show up in the **Plugins** menu. The JAR file contains a manifest that specifies the location where the plugins within it are placed. This specification allows the developer to place the plugin in a specific submenu of the **Plugins** menu, regardless of the folder where the JAR file is placed. This would be especially handy if you create a group of linked or associated plugins that you wish to group within the **Plugins** menu.

Macros folder

The macros folder contains a collection of macros that come with ImageJ and is also the default location to store user-defined macros. ImageJ macros are flat text files with the `.ijm` extension, although this extension is not essential. Any flat text file with valid macro code can be run in ImageJ. Macros in ImageJ have their own language, which is similar to Java, but with a few minor differences. *Chapter 5, Basic Measurements with ImageJ* will investigate how to create macros and will explain the language constructs in ImageJ macros.

Configuring a fresh ImageJ installation

After installing ImageJ, it can be launched for the first time. When using ImageJ, a few settings need to be made to allow successful processing. One of the most important settings is the number of threads and memory available for ImageJ. By default, ImageJ has 512 MB of memory available. This allows for opening images up to 512 MB, which is fine for a large amount of use cases. However, with the current trends in image acquisition, files now tend to be in the range of 1 or more gigabytes. So, one of the first things is to set the memory for ImageJ to at least the size of the largest images you think you'll need to process. Fiji, on the other hand, automatically allocates 50 percent of the available system memory when installed, which can be changed if necessary.

To set the memory allocated to ImageJ, you can set find the setting for memory under **Edit | Options | Memory and Threads....** You can set the maximum memory to any value that is less than the system memory. Keep in mind that on a 32-bit system, it is not possible to allocate more than 3 GB. If you wish to allocate more than 3 GB of memory, installing 64-bit ImageJ on a 64-bit operating system is required.

It is also possible to use a command-line argument to pass the memory size when starting ImageJ. To do so, run ImageJ from the command line using the following command:

```
javaw –Xmx1024m -cp ij.jar ij.ImageJ
```

This tells the computer to run ImageJ with 1024 MB (1024m) of memory. If you need more, then you can change the value of 1024m to whatever value is suitable. However, make sure that you do not use more memory than is available on your system.

Another setting that is important to verify is in the **Appearance** dialog. The **Interpolate zoomed images** option should be unchecked for image processing. This option can interfere or give misleading results when processing:

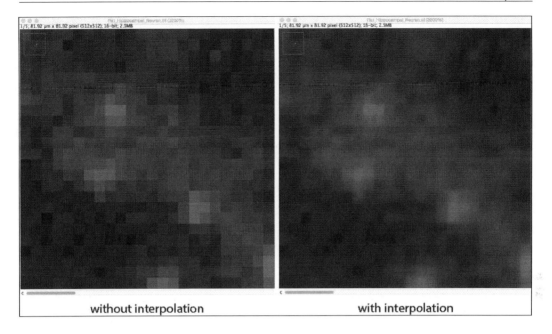

| without interpolation | with interpolation |

If you plan to work with images containing a lot of white pixels, it is also advisable that you change the selection color to a different value than the default Yellow. This can be done via the **Colors** setting in preferences. A good default value in many cases is Orange or Green.

Summary

In this chapter, we looked at the origin and use of ImageJ, and discussed how to download and install it on different platforms. We looked at the basic folder structure of the ImageJ installation and configured it for use. Everything should now be set up to start with the first steps in image processing.

2
Basic Image Processing with ImageJ

After following the instructions in the previous chapter, you should have a working and running installation of ImageJ. This chapter will deal with the following topics:

- Supported image types in ImageJ
- Multidimensional images
- Loading and saving images
- Viewing and obtaining pixel values
- Calibrating images for measurements

Images in ImageJ

ImageJ has a wide support for multiple common image formats such as JPEG, PNG, and TIFF. With the help of the **Bio-Formats** plugin, a wide range of proprietary image formats can also be loaded (for example, STK files [Metamorph], and LSM files [Zeiss]) as well as certain medical image formats (**Dicom**) and astronomy formats (**FITS**). The most recent version of Fiji comes with the Bio-Formats plugin and supports the files of almost all the major image formats.

This chapter will use some of the image files that are available from the sample images item in the **File** menu. These files are accessible from the Internet, so they require a functional Internet connection. The whole suite of images is also available as a single download from the ImageJ website. When using the Fiji distribution, the image set can be cached locally by going to **File | Open Samples | Cache Sample Images** from the menu.

We will start by opening one of these sample images to demonstrate some of the features in ImageJ regarding images. To do so, start ImageJ as described in the previous chapter. Go to **File | Open Samples**, and select **Boats (356K)**. This image is taken from `http://imagej.nih.gov/ij/images/boats.gif`, and shows a picture of some boats in the harbor. The same image can also be loaded by going to **Import | URL** in the **File** menu and copying the earlier URL and pasting it in the field. The image should load and display in a new window as follows:

The title bar shows the filename (**boats.gif**). Just below the title bar is an information strip that shows the key parameters of the image: the size of the image (**720x576 pixels**), the image type (**8 bit**) and the file size (**405K**). The upcoming sections will provide more details on the basics of image types in ImageJ.

Image types

An image is built up using pixels, where each pixel has a value that is encoded by bits. The number of bits determines the number of gray values or colors that can be represented. The upcoming sections will briefly explain the different image types that are supported by ImageJ.

Grayscale images

The boats image from the previous section was an 8-bit grayscale image, which means each pixel has a value between 0 (black) and 255 (white). Grayscale images can also be 16 bit (values between 0 and 65535) and 32 bit (floating-point images). The gray values of an image are represented in the **lookup table (LUT)**. For 8-bit images, the LUT maps a value between 0 and 255 to an equal mix of red, green, and blue on your computer screen to display the gray level. For instance, a mid-gray level of 128 will be displayed on your screen as RGB value (128,128,128). It is also possible to change the mapping of the LUT to different scales for display. By changing the LUT, you can change the color appearance of the image on the screen. If you would like to give the grayscale image a green appearance, you can set the LUT to green. This will tell ImageJ to map the mid-gray value on your screen to the RGB value (0,128,0), thus appearing darker green. The same principles hold for 16-bit and 32-bit images, although they have more levels of gray that they can represent. These distinctions become important when creating macros and plugins, as certain processing steps can only be performed on 8-bit images.

Color images

Color images have generally two bit depths: **8-bit** and **24-bit** color. The 8-bit color image type is an indexed image, where the index determines the color of the image. An example of an 8-bit color image is the GIF file format. It stores up to 256 colors in its index, which results in smaller file sizes at the cost of a reduced number of colors. These images store a table of 256 red, green, and blue (RGB) values (also called the palette). Each entry in the table has an index that is referenced in the image for the pixels that use that specific color. This type is rare nowadays, as the reduced file size is no longer that critical due to larger storage capacity and faster Internet connections. By going to **Image | Color | Show LUT** from the ImageJ menu, you can view the palette or a list of indices from an indexed image.

RGB images such as JPG or PNG files are color images with 24 bits of information: 8 bits each for the red, green, and blue channel. PNG files can have an additional 8 bits for the transparency channel. Besides RGB images, it is also possible to generate images using different color spaces such as **L*a*b** and **HSB**. HSB images split the three components of a RGB image into hue, saturation, and brightness channels. The hue component can be compared to the color (blue, green, violet, and so on) of a pixel. Small hue values are used for red and orange, whereas medium values will represent cyan and blue. High hue values represent magenta and red. In this image, you can see the mapping of the hue channel to colors in an RGB image (the S and B channels were kept white):

Note that the mapping of the hue channel is circular. Both pure white and pure black have the same color. They start at red and end at red.

Modifying the saturation makes the colors more or less *colored*. A small saturation value will make the colors look more gray, while a high saturation value will make the colors more pure. The following example shows a horizontal gradient for the hue channel and a vertical gradient for the saturation channel (the brightness channel was constant; the orange box delineates the different channels):

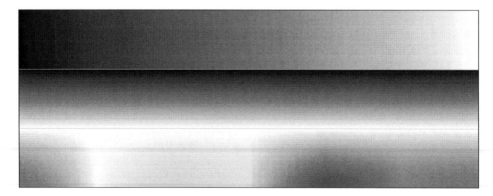

As you move from the bottom of the lower panel to the top, the colors get more washed out, becoming less vibrant and, in this case, becoming white. The color of the upper part is determined by the brightness channel, which was white in this example.

Changing the brightness value makes the colors brighter or darker. High values leave the colors intact and bright, while low values make the colors appear more like black. The following image shows this effect, where the horizontal gradient is again the hue channel, while the vertical gradient is the brightness channel (the saturation channel was uniform white):

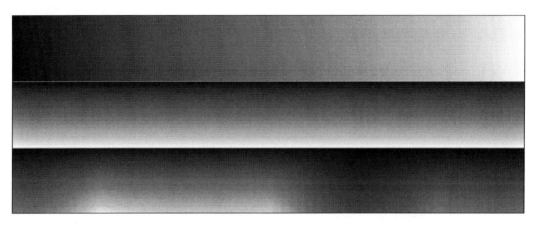

A real image will have combinations of gray values for hue, saturation, and brightness, which together result in the final color.

Converting between image types

It is possible to change a 16-bit image to an 8-bit image at the cost of losing pixel intensity information. To do so, go to **Image | Type** and select the image type you wish to convert to. However, not every conversion is possible. For example, an RGB image cannot be converted to an 8-bit grayscale image (directly)!

Stacks and hyperstacks

The image types described in the previous sections were the basic image types that are supported by most graphical programs. However, ImageJ supports a different class of images that consists of multiple primitive image types combined into a single object: a **stack** or **hyperstack**. The extra dimensions have different names depending on the information they represent. When images are acquired in three dimensions by taking images at multiple levels of a volume, the resulting image is called a **Z-stack**. Each image in a Z-stack is referred to as a slice. When different colors are imaged, the stack is called a multichannel stack, and each image of the stack is called a channel. Finally, there is a stack that holds images that were acquired over time, where each image in the stack is called a frame. A hyperstack is a stack that contains images from more than three dimensions. For instance, a stack with slices, channels, and frames would be a 5D hyperstack. The following sections will briefly explain the different types of stacks and hyperstacks.

Color images and multichannel stacks

Multichannel images contain individual channels that can each have their own color. An RGB image can be converted to a multichannel stack with a channel for red, green, and blue. An example of a multichannel image can be found in the image samples by selecting **Fluorescent Cells (400K)**:

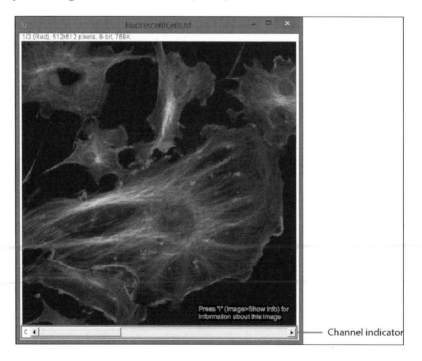

The window looks similar to the **Boats** image. However, there is another bar at the bottom of the image window. This bar has a letter **C** on the left-hand side, indicating that it has multiple channels. Each channel has its own LUT, which, in this case, is Red (channel 1), Green (channel 2), and Blue (channel 3). The bar just below the title bar now also displays some additional image information. It has the current channel indicated out of the total number of channels (1/3), and the color of the text indicates the color of the channel.

This allows for images with 16-bit information for each channel, which allows for images with a total of 48 bits of information in three channels. Internally, ImageJ can handle these files without problems, but most other programs cannot deal with these images. When saving these images, you may need to convert them to a different bit depth to use them in other programs.

ImageJ allows you to change the color of multichannel images using a lookup table. The default is Grays, but other options include Red, Green, Blue, Cyan, Magenta, and Yellow. There are also multicolor LUTs that encode intensity over a range of colors:

The preceding image shows a few examples of a range of LUTs that are available in ImageJ: from left to right green, red, cyan, and spectrum.

Z-stack images and volumes

When making optical sections using a microscope or an MRI machine, the resulting stack will contain information in three dimensions: X, Y, and Z. Each image in this Z-stack is called a slice. Multiple slices form a volume, which can be visualized in 3D. This will be discussed in the next chapter. The appearance of the image will be the same as for a multichannel image. However, instead of **C**, there will be a **Z** next to the slider to indicate that the stack contains slices.

Time series

When taking images at a regular time interval, the resulting stack will be a time series containing an image for each time point called a **frame**. The appearance of the slider will be slightly different. Instead of a letter next to it, there will be a small play button. When you click on it, the time series will play at the speed that the time series was acquired (if the stack was calibrated).

Multidimensional images

Besides multiple channels, frames (for time series) and slices (Z-stacks), it is also possible to combine all three dimensions into a single image file: a 5D image. If you open the **Mitosis (26MB, 5D stack)** sample image, a new window opens with two additional sliders at the bottom of the image window:

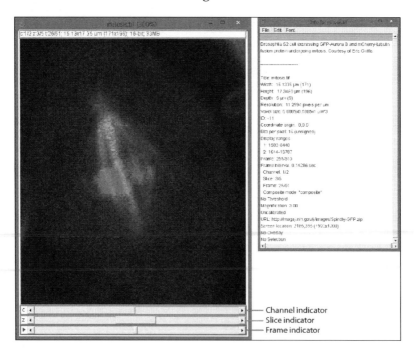

The top slider is again for the channels (indicated by **C**), the middle slider is to navigate the slices (indicated by **Z**), and the last one is to navigate the time frames (indicated by the play button ▶). When you click on the play button, the time series will start playing like a movie, with the speed determined by the time interval between frames. If you wish to change the speed of playback, you can right-click on the play button. Alternatively, you can go to **Image | Stacks | Animation | Animation Options...** from the menu and enter the speed (in frames per second). Larger values mean faster playback.

The bar below the title bar, called the subtitle, again provides additional information. It now shows the selected channel (c:1/2), slice (z:3/5), and frame (t:26/51). This time, the image is also calibrated, and the subtitle also shows the dimensions of the image in micrometers (the size in pixels is indicated between braces).

Extracting image and pixel information

If you wish to have more information about the image, you can press *Ctrl + I* (⌘*+I* on Mac) to get a new window with image information. If you do this for the 5D image, you will get the information shown in the previous image on the right-hand side. This shows a short description of the sample used as well as the dimensions of the image in calibrated units (micrometers) and pixels. It also tells you the bit depth per channel (bits per pixel: 16) and the time interval between frames that was used (frame interval: 0.14286 sec).

The use of the Control key, or ⌘ (command) key on Mac, for shortcuts is optional by default. You can control this by going to **Edit | Options | Misc**. There is a checkbox labeled **Require control/command key for shortcuts**. When selected, the control/command key is required for **the shortcuts** used in ImageJ. When a shortcut requires the **Shift** key as well, this key is still required regardless of the setting! In this book, I will include the control/command key for shortcuts.

To see the value of a pixel, you can place your mouse cursor over the pixel of interest. In the status bar of the ImageJ main window, you can see the following information:

There is information about the location of the pixel (the X and Y coordinates, in calibrated units if the images are calibrated) and the value (intensity or gray value). Coordinates in ImageJ are relative to the upper-left corner (origin). If a Z-stack was loaded, the current z coordinate is also provided. In the next chapter, we will look at other measurements that can be obtained from images.

Note on slice indexing

Note that the value given for the pixel assumes that the first slice is 0, while the information below the title bar assumes that the first slice is 1. When you start developing your own macros and plugins, this distinction can become important!

Loading and saving images

Let's take a look at loading images and sequences in the following sections.

Loading images and sequences

As we have seen, we can load images from a URL by selecting it from the samples or going to **Import | URL** in the **File** menu. For files stored locally on the disk, we can select **File | Open...** and browse to a folder containing our images. It is also possible to drag and drop an image file onto the main ImageJ window to load it. If you drag and drop an entire folder onto the ImageJ window, all the images in that folder will be loaded.

If you have a folder containing individual pictures that you wish to open as a sequence, you can go to **Import | Image Sequence...** in the **File** menu. This allows you to select the first image file of the series, after which ImageJ determines all the images that will be loaded into a single image window. It is possible to use regular expressions to limit the number of images that will be imported.

Importing image sequences

When importing a sequence of images, all the images must be of the same type (bit depth) and have the same dimensions (width and height). If any file has dissimilar dimensions or bit depth, the import will fail and ImageJ will show an error. If other file types are in the same folder that should be ignored for importing, consider placing them in a different folder. Alternatively, you can use the regular expressions field in the import dialog to filter them out.

After the image is loaded, the window shows the filename in the title bar. When a filename is especially long, it may be beneficial to rename the window. Renaming the window can be done by selecting **Image | Rename...** from the menu or by right-clicking on the image and selecting **Rename...** from the context menu.

Saving images

ImageJ allows you to save images to different file types. The preferred file type used by ImageJ is TIFF, as it allows the storage of additional meta-information, regions of interest overlays, and calibration information. ImageJ supports a wide variety of image formats. When you go to **File | Save As**, a list of image formats is presented. The JPEG and PNG formats are compressed formats. They require less disk space for storage. This means they require smaller file sizes depending on the amount of compression that is selected. The TIFF format is a lossless format, but it can support compression.

When saving images, it is important to take into account what the saved image will be used for. When you wish to quantify the image at a later time or you have to repeatedly save it, a lossy compression file format such as JPEG is not recommended. Every time you save the image as a JPEG file, a little quality is lost. Furthermore, JPEG compression is optimized for smooth color gradients, generating artifacts when applied to fluorescent images with abrupt changes in intensity. The following screenshot shows an example that was opened and saved as a JPEG file 200 times. On the left-hand side is the original image, and on the right-hand side is the saved image:

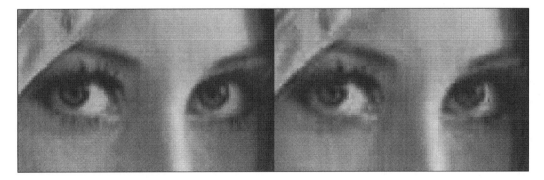

The most apparent problem is around the eyes, where multiple artifacts of the compression can be seen. In the white of the eyes, there are now spots that were not present in the original. The skin also shows a block-like pattern. This is caused by the fact that the JPEG compression is based on blocks of 8 x 8 pixels. In this case, the image was zoomed in to 200 percent, and for a web page, this image might still be acceptable. However, this image would be unacceptable for image quantification due to the artifacts. When you need to save the image many times, or when you are not sure what further processing is required, always save the image as a TIFF file. If you require an image for a web page or presentation, you can use only 8-bit grayscale or RGB images, which can be saved in TIFF, JPG, or PNG.

Image calibration

When you perform image measurements and you wish to measure distances or areas, you need to make sure that your images are calibrated in the proper units. For 2D images or 3D images, you can enter the pixel dimensions, and for time series, you can enter the time interval between frames. To do so, you can press *Ctrl + Shift + P* (⌘ + *Shift + P* on Mac) to display the properties dialog. This allows you to set the unit of measurement (for instance, μm for micrometer) and the values for the width, height, and depth. The values indicate the number of units per pixel. For time series, the frame interval can be entered in seconds. When the **Global** checkbox is checked, this calibration will be applied to all images that are opened.

Viewing images in ImageJ

In order to examine an image in more detail, we may wish to use some of the tools that are available to view images in ImageJ. To show the available tools, let's use the **Fluorescent Cells** images that we opened earlier. The first thing that you may wish to do is look at the detail in the image. This can be done by zooming in on the image by going to **Image | Zoom | In [+]** or by pressing the **+** key. When zooming in, the location of the cursor determines the center of the zoom. The current zoom level is indicated in the image title bar, and the maximum zoom level is 3200 percent. When you zoom in, the window rescales until it no longer fits on the desktop. When you zoom in beyond that point, the window size stays the same and the location of the current zoom is indicated in the top-left corner as an overlay:

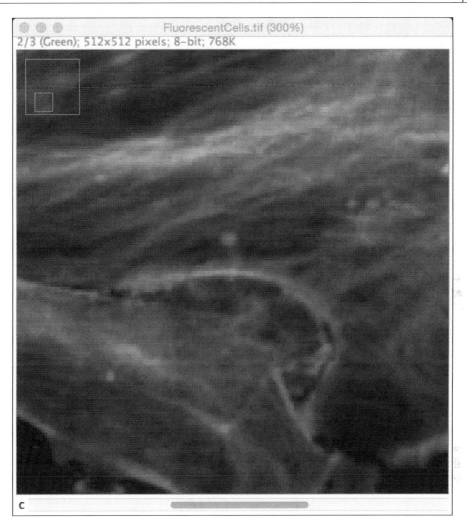

The large blue square represents the entire image, while the small square inside indicates the current position of the zoomed display (in this case, at the lower-left side of the image). To zoom out, select **Image | Zoom | Out [-]** from the menu or use the - key.

If you notice that the zoomed image shows some artifacts as shown in the following image, make sure you disabled **Interpolate zoomed images** by going to **Edit | Options | Appearance…**, as described in the first chapter:

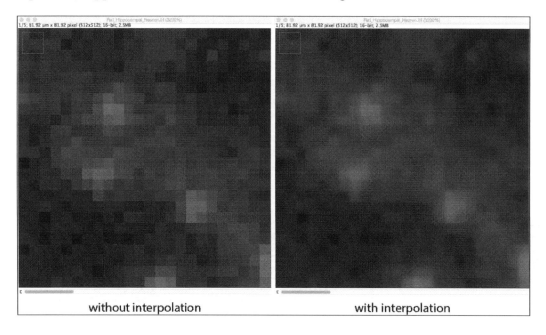

without interpolation   with interpolation

Sometimes, when you acquire images, the exposure settings are suboptimal. This means you are not using the entire range of gray values available. In order to still see the signal, you can adjust the brightness and contrast of the image. To do so, select **Image | Adjust | Brightness/Contrast** from the menu or press *Ctrl + Shift + C*. This adjustment is non-destructive. It does not change the values in the image file until you press **Apply** in the **Brightness/Contrast** dialog for 8 and 16-bit images. The **Apply** button does not work for 32-bit images. If you press **Reset**, the values are restored to the initial values or to the values that were set after **Apply** was pressed. If you have an underexposed (dark) image, you can make it brighter by lowering the **Maximum** slider or increasing the **Brightness** slider.

Brightness/Contrast adjustments and measurements

When you adjust the **Brightness/Contrast** of an image and apply it, the gray values of the image are irreversibly modified. If you still wish to perform measurements that include intensity values, applying the modifications would alter your results (and perhaps, conclusions). Only use the **Apply** button when you create an image for non-critical viewing (presentations) or when measuring lengths or areas independent of intensity.

Viewing multichannel images

When you have a multichannel image, you may sometimes want to hide channels from being viewed. ImageJ allows you to show or hide any channel in a multichannel image by going to **Image | Color | Channels Tool...** in the menu or by pressing *Ctrl + Shift + Z*. A dialog opens with a checkbox for each channel. When the box is checked, the channel is displayed. Otherwise, it is switched off (hidden). It is also possible to change the order of the channels by going to **Image | Color | Arrange Channels...**. When modifying the **Brightness/Contrast** of a multichannel image, the adjustments are only applied to the current channel that is displayed. The currently selected channel can be checked on the info bar directly underneath the title bar. The color of the histogram in the **Brightness/Contrast** dialog also reflects the channel color selected.

Brightness/Contrast adjustments and the Channels Tool

When you have hidden channels using the **Channels Tool**, they can still be modified by the **Brightness/Contrast** dialog. If the hidden channel is currently selected when you modify the **Brightness/Contrast**, the adjustments would be made by ImageJ, but are not visible. Always verify the current channel before making adjustments!

Viewing time series

When viewing time series, adjustments for brightness and contrast are visible in all frames of the time series. If you wish to apply an adjustment, ImageJ will ask whether you wish to do so for the current frame or for all the frames. When you apply the settings to all the frames, the adjustment is equal for all frames, irrespective of the intensity in the frame. This means that this does not help for time series that show a decrease in fluorescence over time (that is, bleaching). Bleaching is inherent in fluorescence imaging and causes a decrease in intensity over time. Generally speaking, this effect follows an exponential decay trend. Fiji has an option to correct this bleaching process by selecting **Image | Adjust | Bleach Correction** from the menu. For most time series that experience bleaching, the best correction method to select is **Exponential Fit**. This method is more robust against changes in intensity from sources other than bleaching. If the cause for the change in intensity is different, you may want to use the **Simple Ratio** method to correct the time series. Running this correction results in a new image window with the corrected data, which means that the original remains unaltered.

Summary

In this chapter, we discussed the different image types that are supported by ImageJ. You also saw how to load images from a disk or from a URL. We looked at the anatomy of an image window in ImageJ and the information that can be viewed. We applied a calibration to images in order to prepare for length and area measurements. Finally, we looked at different ways of viewing different image types. You learned how to adjust the brightness and contrast of the images.

In the next chapter, we will look at ways to perform basic processing steps using the ImageJ interface.

3

Advanced Image Processing with ImageJ

The previous chapter showed you how to load and view images in ImageJ and how to make basic alterations to image intensity and pixel values. This chapter will deal with the techniques used to preprocess images. We will prepare them for image analysis and measurements. This chapter will apply some of the techniques we examined in the earlier chapters. We will cover the following topics:

- Correcting images
- Z-stack processing
- Time series processing
- Image and stack calculations

Correcting images

In order to analyze images, we sometimes need to correct the problems that were present during acquisition. Problems such as noise, uneven illumination, and background fluorescence can cause many issues during image analysis. I will provide a little technical background on the sources of these problems and then follow this up with how they can be corrected in ImageJ.

Technical background

Of the many sources of noise that exist in imaging, a few can be corrected with correct acquisition settings. Others are inherent in the electronics and physical properties of the camera, and cannot be easily fixed. I will first deal with the source of noise that can be remedied with optimizing acquisition: **Shot** or **Poisson** noise. Next, we will look at **Electronic** or **Dark** noise.

Correcting Shot noise

Shot noise is caused by the physical properties of light; light can be seen as packages of light or photons. The number of photons that are collected by each photo-detector site on the camera determines the final pixel intensity. If only a few photons hit the detector at any time, the differences in the number of photons could be large. This is called a Poisson process, and the signal-to-noise ratio can be expressed as follows:

$$SNR = \frac{N}{\sqrt{N}}$$

This means that the **signal-to-noise ratio** (**SNR**) will get larger as the number of photons (*N*) increases. By increasing the exposure time or the illumination intensity, the number of photons per pixel and the SNR will increase. A low SNR cannot be fixed with processing techniques in software.

Correcting dark noise

Another source of noise is called dark noise or dark current. This source of noise comes from the electronics in the camera and can be visualized by taking an image with the camera without illumination. In digital consumer cameras, exposing the image while the lens is completely covered can easily do this. You can even try it with the camera of your phone. Just cover the lens tightly and take a picture (make sure the flash is disabled!). As an example, the following figure shows a small region of an image taken by two different cameras, both with the same settings. The left-hand image is a small region of an image taken with a Sony α6000 (2014), while the image on the right-hand side is from a Canon EOS 550D (2010). The orange bar is there to delineate them:

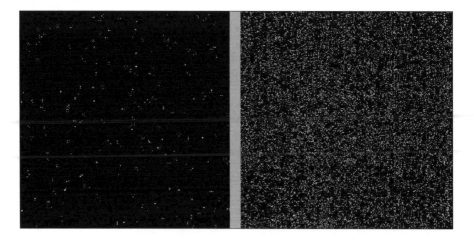

The intensities of each image were equalized to show the pattern, and only the green channel is shown in this example. The settings for both cameras were as follows: 1/10sec exposure, *f*5.6, and ISO 200. It is clear from these images that the noise level from the electronics is quite different between the two camera sensors. Note that most scientific cameras, especially cooled **EM-CCD (Electron-Multiplying CCD)** cameras, have far lower levels of electronic noise. This allows some EM-CCD cameras to detect single photons and even count them.

In order for the subtraction of the dark noise signal to work, the exposure duration needs to be identical to the exposure time during the acquisition to get the same level of dark noise. The duration of the exposure is directly linked to the amount of noise. A longer exposure results in more dark noise. This type of noise can be easily fixed in ImageJ using the image calculator that will be introduced a little later in this chapter.

To determine the noise level of your own camera, take a picture with the lens covered (make sure it is completely blocked from all light). Ideally, you should do this with your camera capturing images as RAW files. When a camera acquires images as JPEG files, the camera already performs some noise reduction on the image. If you can only capture images in JPEG, check to see whether there is an option to switch off the noise reduction. Now, open the image in ImageJ, as was illustrated in the previous chapter, and follow these steps:

1. Select your darkshot image window by clicking on it, making it active. In ImageJ, most commands will operate on the active image, or the last opened image. By clicking on an image window, that image becomes the active image.

2. In order to determine the noise level, we can select an area that we want to measure. We will create a rectangle by specifying it by entering the specific values. To do this, go to **Edit | Selection | Specify...** and select the **Centered** checkbox, before entering 512 for the width and height. For the **X coordinate** and **Y coordinate**, enter half the width and height of your image (indicated in the image subtitle) and click on **OK**.

3. Make sure that the measurements are set to standard deviation. This can be done by going to **Analyze | Set Measurements** and selecting the **Standard deviation** checkbox. Selecting other parameters for measurement is fine, and in the output below **Area**, **Mean gray value** and **Min & max gray value** were also selected. For this exercise, the **Standard deviation** option is the only relevant parameter that is required.

4. Perform the measurement by pressing *Ctrl + M* or by going to **Analyze | Measure**. You can measure regions immediately after placing them, or you can add them to the **ROI Manager** (see the next chapter for more details) before measuring them.

The results should now be visible in a new window labeled **Results**. Depending on which parameters you selected, the results in this window might deviate from the one shown here (I have included area and the minimum and maximum values):

	Area	Mean	StdDev	Min	Max
1	262144	0.0039	0.0639	0	4
2	262144	0.1914	0.4070	0	11

The first line contains the results from the α6000 camera, and the second line contains the results from the EOS 550D camera. The area is identical (*512 x 512 = 262144 pixels*) for both measurements, but the standard deviation (a measure of the noise) is lower for the first camera by a factor of 6.3. Also, the mean of the first camera is closer to 0, as you would expect the value to be when there is no light hitting the sensor.

> Cameras can have pixels that no longer work (**dead pixels**). Dead pixels will show as black pixels in bright areas and always occur at the same location. The opposite can also happen. Very bright pixels in dark areas are called **hot pixels**. Hot pixels do not have to occur at the same location every time and are more common with very long exposure times. For EMCCD cameras, there is another source of bright pixels, which is caused by cosmic rays hitting the image sensor. These events are relatively common in long time series, and present themselves as very bright regions for only a single frame. The removal of dead and hot pixels follows the same methodology as the dark noise removal.

For most type of exposures, these levels of noise are so small that they do not cause degradation of your pictures. A picture at the beach with the sun in the sky will not require correction. With the enormous amount of light that is detected, the electronic noise is drowned out completely. However, one field of image acquisition where dark noise is a substantial factor is in the field of astrophotography or night-time photography. Whenever long exposures are required for image acquisition, the electronic noise becomes a substantial factor that can degrade your image.

To reduce the effects of sensor noise in low-light conditions, you need to change the way you acquire your image slightly: instead of a single exposure, you need multiple exposures in quick succession. Some cameras support this automatically, using names such as handheld twilight (Sony) or multi-frame noise reduction (Pentax, Olympus etc.). In this mode you take 2 or more pictures in rapid succession and the final image is an average of the series of images. You can also do something like this in ImageJ by using the following procedure:

1. Open the multiple images that you acquired in succession (make sure there are no other images opened!)

2. Select **Image | Stacks | Images to Stack** from the menu. You will now have a single window where every slice represents one image that you took.

3. Create the noise-reduction image by selecting **Image | Stacks | Z Project...** from the menu and use Average Intensity as the projection type.

A thing to keep in mind is the following: when anything moves between the individual exposures, this method will not provide good results. It is possible to correct for simple shifts, but this only works in the simplest of cases.

Uneven illumination – background subtraction

When an image is acquired under difficult lighting conditions, it can sometimes occur that the illumination is not even across the image sensor. This effect of uneven illumination is something that can easily be corrected in ImageJ. To show how this is done, we will take an image acquired with brightfield illumination on an inverted microscope using **Differential Interference Contrast (DIC)** optics.

DIC images provide contrast by looking at the difference in thickness of your specimen. A single light wave is split into two separate rays that are slightly separated but parallel and with the same phase. When one ray goes through an object with higher density than the parallel ray, the waves will shift out of phase. When they are recombined, the out-of-phase rays will partially cancel each other out (interference). This results in less light on the camera pixel, making the pixel darker. For cells, the strongest interference can be found close to the membrane of the cell. One ray will pass through the cell, while the parallel ray will pass through the water outside the cell.

The image shows the effect of uneven illumination. The left-hand side of the frame is darker than the middle, and the gradient runs along the frame in a slightly diagonal direction. It is also clear that the field is not going in one direction. The middle is the brightest and the two edges, left and right, are darker:

As a first attempt, we will use the background subtraction method to see whether this will fix the problem. To do so, we need to go to **Process | Subtract Background...** and use the following settings:

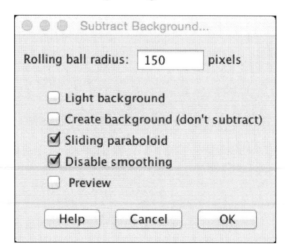

After applying the background subtraction, the image is altered, but the effect of the uneven background is still not fixed. The image is actually a little darker on the left-bottom side, and also the middle did not decrease in intensity that much (see the left-hand-side image). Note that when the **Light background** option was selected (see the right-hand-side image), there is a strong over compensation on both the left and right-hand sides. Not only is the contrast reduced on those sides, but also the illumination is now more uneven than it was before the correction:

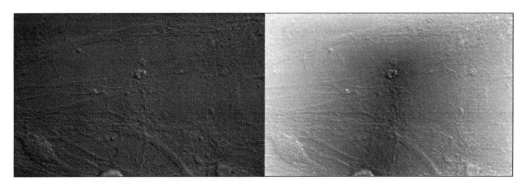

Disabling the **Sliding paraboloid** option also caused artifacts that were even more artificial and incorrect. The problem with this type of background subtraction is that it assumes a homogeneously decreasing change in background. This means that the changes in background should be smooth and go from high to low in a single direction (left to right, diagonal, and so on.). However, DIC images such as this one have a tendency to have a background that has more of a U-shape: high at the edges and low in the middle, or vice versa. Therefore, this method is unsuitable for this type of image, and other methods need to be explored to fix this problem.

Next, we will try to eliminate the background using a method called pseudo-flatfield correction. This method is based on filtering the image using a Gaussian filter that blurs the details. This filter will capture the uneven illumination and separate it from the objects in the frame. The basis of how these filters work will be discussed in the next chapter in more detail. Let's create the background image that we will use to correct the uneven illumination. You need to perform the following steps:

1. First, we want to duplicate the image so that we keep the original image for subtraction. To do so, we will go to **Image | Duplicate...** or use *Ctrl + Shift + D* and name the duplicate image `background`.

2. To create a Gaussian low-pass filter, we will select the background image and go to **Process | Filters | Gaussian Blur...**, entering a value of `150` for the sigma (radius). When you check the preview checkbox, you will see that the image will look like it is defocused. You can see that the objects can no longer be distinguished, and what is left is the diagonal background illumination.

3. We can now subtract this background from the original image to correct the uneven illumination. To do this, we will start the image calculator by going to **Process | Image Calculator...** from the menu. Then, we will select the original image as **Image1** and the background image as **Image2**. Set the operation to **Subtract** and check the **Create new window** and **32-bit (float) result** checkboxes. The following image shows the effect of the subtraction and how it corrected the uneven illumination:

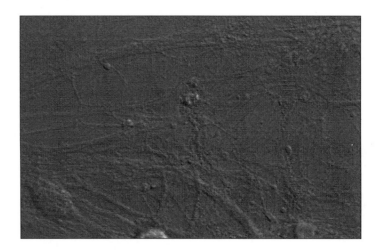

Image normalization

To enhance the contrast of an underexposed image, you can go to **Process | Enhance Contrast...** option, and select the **Normalize** checkbox. This stretches the gray values over the entire range of an 8-bit or 16-bit image. It does not work on RGB images. The following image shows the effect of the normalization, with the original image on the left-hand side and the normalized image on the right-hand side:

This also works for stacks or time series, where the normalization can be done for each frame separately. A similar effect can be obtained using the **Auto** option in the **Brightness/Contrast** window, as described in the previous chapter. Note that the normalization is applied to the image and modifies the pixel values irreversibly. If the signal should not change over time, this should not pose a big problem for measurements. However, for intensity changes over time, this method will distort or remove the changes.

Bleach correction

When imaging fluorescence, the illumination can cause the bleaching of the fluorophore under investigation. This effect is well established and is related to the intensity of the excitation light. To avoid this effect, it is better to use a long exposure with low intensity light. However, this may not always be possible. The amount of bleaching is related to the intensity at the beginning and decreases in an exponential fashion. To see whether an image series is affected by bleaching, we can make a quick measurement on the entire image for each frame to see what the mean intensity is. Note that if there are changes in illumination or background signal in individual frames, the results might not look like a smooth curve. To make a quick measurement, press *Ctrl + A* to select the entire frame and then press *Ctrl + M* to measure the intensity. Repeat the measurement for each frame and plot the mean intensity values against the frame number (or time, if you know the interval) in your favorite graphics program. In this case, I used **MATLAB** to create the plot, although you could also create the plot by selecting **Image | Stacks | Plot Z-axis Profile** from the menu in ImageJ. Here is an example of a bleaching curve:

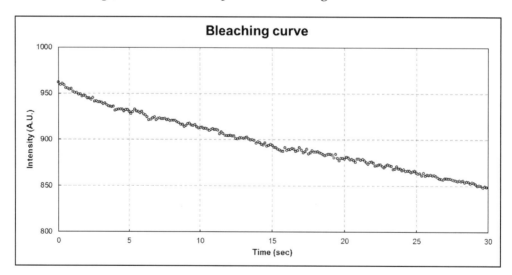

This collection of points seems to follow a trend that is close to either a straight line or an exponential curve, although the trend in the first 2 seconds seems more exponential than linear.

In order to perform bleach correction, you can select the correction plugin in Fiji by going to **Image | Adjust | Bleach Correction**. There are three methods for correction:

- Simple ratio
- Exponential fit
- Histogram matching

Simple ratio is the best method if the decrease in intensity does not follow a regular shape, such as an exponential decay function. For most fluorescence imaging, this method yields good results and can be combined with fluorescence measurements. The histogram matching method performs better with noisy images, but is less suitable for intensity measurements.

Since our trend looked more like an exponential decay model, we selected the second method, which fits a single exponential function to the data:

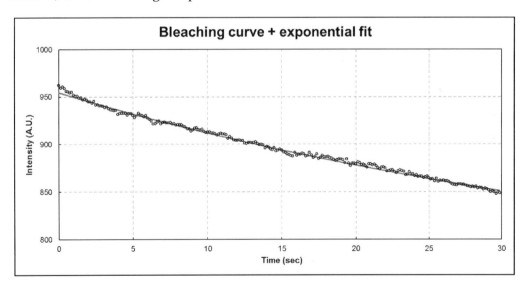

This plot was generated using the parameters obtained by the **bleach correction** command and entering them in MATLAB. The ImageJ command itself also generates a plot with the data and the fitted curve. However, the axes are labeled X and Y. So, for the purpose of clarity, I have recreated the plot with the correct labels. The red line indicates the fitted function, which matches the curve with an R^2 value of .9954 (a very good fit). The model consists of three parameters, labeled a, b, and c. The value of a indicates how much above the asymptote, indicated by the c value, the first point lies. The asymptote is the value to which this exponential curve will go when given infinite time. The value of b indicates the rate at which the curve decays. If you want to know the time it takes to lose half of the initial fluorescence, you can use the following formula, using the b value from the fitting:

$$t_{1/2} = \frac{\ln(2)}{b}$$

The preceding formula gives you the half-time of the fluorescence loss. Note that the b parameter for the fit is expressed in frames and not time. So, when using the preceding formula, you need to multiply the result with your frame interval to get the value in seconds (or minutes). In the graph shown earlier, the half-time is 30.587 seconds (using the formula with a b value of 0.0028327 and a frame interval of 0.125 seconds).

Stack processing

ImageJ is very suitable to process information that has more than two dimensions: data acquired at different Z-levels or at different time points. We have already seen an example of stack processing in the section on noise correction. The next section will deal with time series consisting of frames. However, first, we will explore more options when dealing with image stacks containing slices (Z-stacks).

Processing Z-stacks

Z-stacks are series of 2D images that were acquired at different heights or distances. In a microscope, this is done by moving the objective or the stage up or down and acquiring an image at specific intervals. In **Magnetic Resonance Imaging (MRI)**, this is done by moving the patient through the center of the scanner. The scanner then creates an image for each position using radio pulses that create fluctuations in the magnetic field. These fluctuations can be measured by the detector in an MRI machine. This results in a single slice that can be combined into a single file. Some of the processing that you may want to perform on this type of image involves creating projections or 3D renders of the volume. We will first examine the projections that you can create. Then, you will understand why you would create them.

Stack projections

We have already seen an example of a Z-projection in the section on noise cancellation. In the previous section, we used the projection to create an average intensity for each pixel over the frames. For images that contain slices (Z-information), an average projection is usually not the most useful projection. However, there are other Z-projections available in ImageJ that are more applicable for Z-stacks. The following sections will deal with some examples of these projections.

Maximum projection

A maximum projection uses the maximum intensity of each pixel across the slices. If a stack has 20 slices, then each pixel will contain the maximum value across the 20 slices. This type of projection can be helpful to reduce the third dimension of a Z-stack in order to create a two-dimensional representation of the data. This type of projection essentially flattens the image. When used on fluorescence images with sparse signal (few bright pixels) at the same location, this projection has the effect of showing all the objects in a single frame. It is also useful for fluorescent images that have thin objects that are in focus in different slices at different positions. By flattening the Z-stack, all the in-focus parts will be visible in one continuous shape. You can visualize this as a flight of stairs. Each step has a different Z-position, but if you would flatten the steps (assuming that the steps do not overlap), you would get a rectangular board. If you have an image that is not sparse, then this projection would be of little use. To demonstrate this projection, open the **Confocal Series** image from the sample images. Go to **Image | Stacks | Z Project...** and choose **Max Intensity** as the projection type. The following image shows the result of this projection:

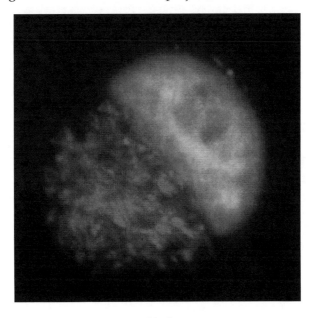

As is visible in the preceding image, the maximum intensity projection shows the entire shape of the cell, but some information was lost. Specifically, the small details in the first frames are drowned out by the intense pixels from the middle of the volume. For some representations, this is fine. For some Z-stacks, the rough shape of the total volume is unclear in the individual slices, but the maximum projection shows the general shape.

To demonstrate this effect, we will open the **Bat Cochlea Volume** image by going to **File | Open Samples**. Looking at a few slices from this volume gives very little information about the shape of this sensory organ (the numbers indicate the slice number):

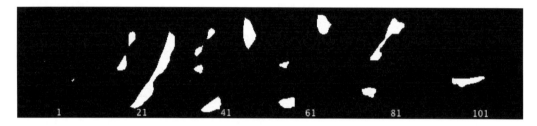

When we create a maximum intensity projection, the general shape of this organ becomes much more obvious: it is shaped like a twisted spiral (the cochlea is the shell-shaped cavity that is used for hearing). When you also open the **Bat Cochlea Renderings** image by going to **File | Open Samples**, you see the 3D rendering of the volume:

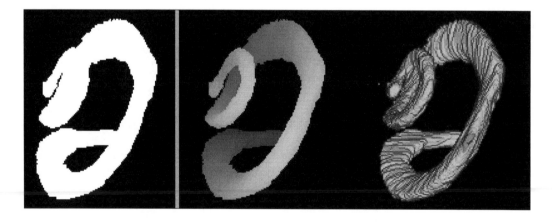

The image on the left-hand side shows the maximum projection of the Z-stack, while the images on the right-hand side show the rendered volumes. From this image, it is clear that the maximum projection provides more information than the individual slices. However, some of the details are still lost in the process. In particular the top-left part of the cochlea is very unclear in the maximum projection. The start of the spiral is obscured because of the loop behind it.

Fiji has an option that allows you to create a maximum projection that contains more information: depth coding. Depth coding assigns a color to the Z-location of a pixel, resulting in different colors for different slices. To do so in Fiji, go to **Image | Hyperstacks | Temporal-Color Code** and select **Grays** for the LUT. This results in the middle representation in the preceding image (not exactly, but very similar). Note that you will get a message that the slices and frames were swapped. This is done because this plugin is designed for time series and not Z-stacks. The right image in the preceding figure is a 3D rendering of the volume, which will be covered in the next section.

Volume viewing and rendering

When images are acquired over a range of depths, the goal is usually to view this collection of images as a 3D volume. Another useful viewing aspect is to take a 3-dimensional volume, cut it along the *z* axis, and view the volume from the side. This latter view cannot be obtained from the two-dimensional images. For this example, we will use two different stacks from the sample images. Let's start with viewing the volume of an MRI stack. To open the image, go to **File | Open Samples** and select **MRI stack**. This is an MRI stack where every slice is at a different level through the head (the numbers indicate the slice number):

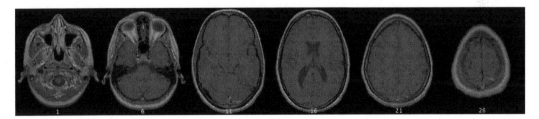

The eyes are clearly visible in slice number 6 as two dark orbs on the top of the image. Slice 11 shows the brain within the skull, and frame 16 shows the ventricles as black holes in the middle of the head. Slice 26 shows the top of the head. The area is much smaller indicating that the crown of the head is being reached.

A lot of information is already present in the slices. The eyes can clearly be seen, as well as the sinuses and the nose (slice 1). The information in these slices is not complete, however. We lack shape along the *z* axis. To view the three-dimensional shape of this volume, we can use a viewer that comes with Fiji. Go to **Plugins | Volume Viewer** with the MRI stack selected. If you have the standard ImageJ, the **Volume Viewer** plugin can be downloaded and installed from the plugins page. Then, the following window will open:

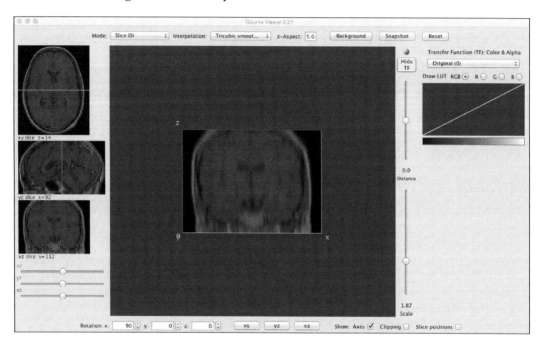

This is **Volume Viewer**, which is included in Fiji and available as a plugin for ImageJ. On the left-hand side, there are three images that show different views of the volume: an **xy** slice (this is the top view for this stack), a **yz** slice (this is a side view for this stack), and finally, an **xz** slice (this is a front view for this stack). The large image in the middle of the viewer is the current selected view, in this case, the *xz* slice view. The position of this slice is indicated in the overview images on the left-hand side by the cyan (*xy*) and green (**yz**) lines. Note that I adjusted the **z-Aspect** by entering 5 and pressing *Enter* instead of the value of 1 based on the current calibration. The volume, otherwise, looks very squashed. The squashed appearance is caused by the fact that this image was not calibrated. Each voxel (a contraction of volume and pixel) is 1 x 1 x 1, without a unit. A typical value for the voxel size in MRI images is 1.5 x 1.5 x 3.0 mm, which can be set using the image properties as described in the previous chapter. We can now change the view by selecting the view buttons at the bottom of the viewer. The **yz** button will give us a side view of this volume. It is also possible to rotate the volume by clicking and dragging the mouse.

The size of the volume viewer window has a minimum size of ±1024 x 768 pixels. This can mean that depending on the pixel dimensions of your monitor, some of the controls might fall off the screen. For most modern displays, this should not be an issue. However, for some small screens or beamers, this can be a problem.

Next, we will look at a different type of image: a Z-stack of a fly brain using fluorescent imaging. To open the image, go to **File | Open Samples** and select the **Fly Brain** image. The Z-stack will open, and you can go through the slices:

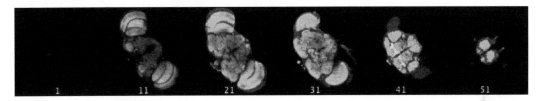

The first slice contains no bright pixels, but as you move through the stack, the brain of the fruit fly starts to show defined features. This stack shows the brain from a (rotated) front view in contrast to the MRI stack, which was displayed as a top view. We will use the volume viewer to examine the entire volume and use it to create a short movie of the volume turning. To start, select the **Fly Brain** stack and go to **Plugins | Volume Viewer**. The initial image will be a slice view, but for this example, we want to switch to a different mode. Select **Volume (4)** mode using the selector at the top of the viewer. We will set the interpolation to **Tricubic sharp (3)** using the drop-down selector. On the right-hand side of the viewer, we will modify the transfer function to **2D Grad** to create a slightly more pleasing view. Next, we will set the rotation for X, Y, and Z at the bottom of the volume viewer to -90, 30, and 180 respectively. This will provide a side view of the brain.

By pressing the **Snapshot** button (top right) in the viewer, we will get a picture of the current view. Next, we will increase the value for the Y rotation with 10-degree increments and take a snapshot every time until you have reached 210 degrees. We now made snapshots of the brain from one side of the brain to the other side (180 degrees). To turn this into an animation, all we have to do is go to **Image | Stacks | Images to Stack**. If you close the original stack, you only have to press OK in the dialog. Otherwise, you would have to enter `Volume_Viewer` in the **Title contains** field. You will now have a stack that can be played and saved as a movie for presentation purposes. For this example, we used increments of 10 degrees for the rotation, which gives an adequate result. However, if you take smaller increments, the result will look much smoother. Feel free to modify the angles at which you view the volume for different results as well as experiment with the other settings available within the volume viewer.

The volume viewer is a very powerful function in ImageJ that allows for the investigation and visualization of 3D objects. Use the **Slice (0)** mode to examine the volume as a cross-section and the **Volume (4)** mode to see a solid model.

Processing time series

Time series consists of images acquired over time, usually with a fixed interval. Movies can also be seen as time series with a fixed interval of 24 or 25 frames per second (**fps**). Processing of time series mostly focuses on two areas: fluctuations in intensity over time and background reduction and normalization. Fluctuations in intensity have been covered in the previous section where we looked at bleach correction. In the following section, we will look at ways to normalize the time series data.

Normalizing time series data

Normalizing time series data will help in further analysis by providing a correction for the baseline intensity. Many times, the goal of time series is to look at changes in intensity or movement over time. Normalizing will yield cleaner time series data relative to the resting or baseline state. A very simple normalization is to calculate ΔF over F0 (dFF0). The basis for this metric is that the baseline fluorescence can be different between time series, but the changes in intensity *relative to the baseline* are similar. It is calculated using the following formula:

$$dFF0 = \frac{\Delta F}{F_0}$$

$$\Delta F = F_t - F_0, \qquad F_0 = \frac{\sum_{i=1}^{n} F_i}{n}$$

The numerator is the difference between the current frame (Ft) and the baseline (F0). The baseline is the average of the first n frames. A value of *dFF0* larger than 1 indicates the signal increased relative to the baseline, while a value less than 1 indicates a decrease relative to the baseline. It is possible to perform this calculation only on the measured values of a time series (in Excel or MATLAB), but you can also transform the time series directly. I will now show you how to do this in ImageJ using the Z projection, image duplication, and image calculator.

To get started, we will open the `timeseries_events.tif` image, which is available in the online resources with this book. This is a time series of vesicles in a cell that are transported and fuse when the cell is stimulated with electrodes. It contains two channels: one with a red fluorescent marker and the other with a green fluorescent marker. The red marker is fluorescent at all times until the vesicle fuses, at which point it disappears. The green marker is not fluorescent while the cargo is within the vesicle, but as soon as it fuses, it becomes bright. To start the processing, we first want to split the channels into two different time series. To do this, select the time series and go to **Image | Color | Split Channels** to generate two time series: one for each channel. We will select the green channel, which was labeled `C1_timeseries_events.tif`, using the **split channels** command.

We can now start with the first step in the creation of the dFF0 time series: creating the baseline frame. We will go to **Image | Stacks | Z Project...** and set the method to **Average Intensity** and **Stop slice:** to 5. What we do here is create an average of the first five frames. This effectively reduces the noise in the individual frames by averaging it out while leaving the bright objects present in the first frames intact. Let's rename the resulting image to make it easier to identify later on. Right-click on the average image and select **Rename...** from the context menu. Rename the image to F0 so that it will be easy to select later on.

For the next step, we will create the ΔF image. As explained at the beginning of this section, this image is the raw image minus the baseline image. To get this image, we will use the image calculator by going to **Process | Image Calculator** from the **ImageJ** menu. Select the original time series as `Image1` and the **F0** image as `Image2`. Then, set the method to **Subtract**. Make sure that the **Create new window** option is selected.

> The order of the images is very important when one of them is a stack or time series and the other is a single frame. The stack always needs to be set at the `Image1` position if you wish to modify each slice or frame. For subtraction, this is usually obvious, but for multiplication, the order of the operation would not be important from a mathematical perspective (*A* × *B equals B* × *A*). However, if you place the time series or stack on `Image2` and the single frame on `Image1`, only the current slice or frame is used for the calculation!

We now have the ΔF stack, so let's rename it to make it easier. Right-click on the new time series, select **Rename...**, and enter deltaF as the new name.

Now, we can create the final time series that is normalized to the baseline. Note that the `deltaF` series by itself already provides an improvement over the original time series as it is corrected for the initial static background. To create the *dFF0* image, we will use the Image Calculator again. This time, we will select `deltaF` as `Image1` and `F0` as `Image2` and the **Divide** operation. Select the **Create new window** and **32-bit (float) result** options.

> This time, the 32-bit result option is useful. As we noted earlier, in the definition of the calculation, we expected the results to be between 0 and infinity. This is denoted as $[0, \infty]$ in mathematical notation. This means that that any value, including 0 and infinity, are within the range of possible values. When this option is not selected during the calculation, all the values below 1 will be rounded to 0, and information about these events are lost. Note that for the example used here, the events we wish to see will have a value larger than 1. So, in this particular case, it is not crucial.

The new image is now the dFF0 image, which has been corrected for the baseline and normalized to the initial baseline intensity. The following image shows the effect of this normalization (second row), compared to the original images (first row):

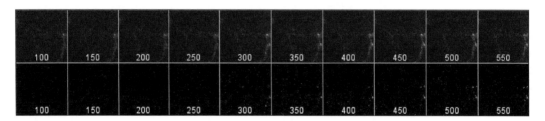

The clearest difference that can be seen is that the images before frame **300** are nearly black, indicating that nothing is happening relative to the baseline situation. At frame **300** and beyond, the increase in signal at different locations is very clear, indicating that the signal has increased in these locations.

Summary

In this chapter, we investigated the processing of different types of images. We looked at different sources of noise that can corrupt images and degrade their quality. You learned how to apply different corrections to the images to fix these problems. We then looked at processing steps specifically aimed at Z-stacks and time series.

In the next chapter, we will see how to separate pixels into different groups and how to clean up and filter the result for further processing.

4

Image Segmentation and Feature Extraction with ImageJ

The previous chapter looked at processing images to view and correct imperfections in acquisition. This chapter will introduce techniques for segmenting images and extracting features that are relevant for processing and analysis. The following topics will be covered in this chapter:

- Image segmentation
- Morphological processing
- Image filtering and convolution
- Feature extraction

Image segmentation

For many steps in image analysis, it is important to split the image into two separate (non-overlapping) components. These components are usually labeled as background and foreground. Generally speaking, the background is the part of the image we are not directly interested in when we analyze the image. We normally restrict our analysis to parts of the image that are deemed as the foreground. This splitting into two components is called segmentation and is primarily based on pixel intensity. This is important if you wish to count and measure a number of unique objects of a specific type or measure the intensity of a single complex object while excluding the background from the measurement.

Image thresholding

To achieve the split of an image into background and foreground, we will set a threshold value. Values below this threshold will be classified as one group, while pixels with higher or equal values will be classified as another group. In general, the background in fluorescent images contains values close to black (that is, a dark background), while brightfield images have background values closer to white (a light background). The output of thresholding is an image called a mask in ImageJ, which is a binary image. Its pixels have only two values (0 and 255).

We will look at how to perform basic thresholding on a grayscale image first. After that, we will look at the possibilities for thresholding a color image. The difference between these two image types stems from the fact that a color image does not have an easy way of setting a threshold. Each pixel contains three values (red, green, and blue), and a single threshold value does not segment the image in useful ways generally.

Thresholding grayscale images

We will start by taking a grayscale image from the sample images and segmenting it. For this example, we will use the **Blobs** image. Thresholding would be the first step if you wanted to measure the size of each individual blob as well as get a count of the number of blobs in the image. Note that for small images such as this example, counting could be done by hand. However, if you need to do this for a large number of images, this method of counting by hand would be very tedious.

To set a threshold, go to **Image | Adjust | Threshold...** or press *Ctrl + Shift + T*. The threshold dialog will open with a few options:

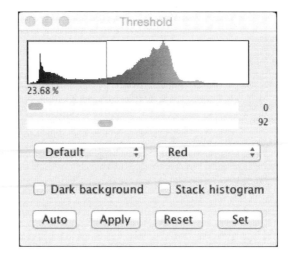

For fluorescent images, the **Dark background** checkbox needs to be selected, while for brightfield images, it needs to be deselected (unless you use darkfield illumination methods). The methods available can be set in the drop-down list on the left-hand side. The default method is based on the **IsoData** method. The **IsoData** method determines the value of the threshold based on the following procedure:

- Take an initial value for the threshold T
- Calculate the average intensity of the background (BG) and the foreground (FG) pixels based on the value of T
- If the average of BG and FG in step *ii* is not equal to T, increment the threshold value T and repeat step *ii*

For more information and references on thresholding methods, refer to the Fiji website at `http://fiji.sc/Auto_Threshold#Available_methods` for an overview. The drop-down list on the right-hand side gives the option to show the effect of the thresholding. When **Red** is selected, the foreground selection is displayed as red while the background stays in grayscale.

Once you have the threshold set, you can create a binary image by pressing **Apply** in the threshold window or by going to **Edit | Selection | Create Mask**. The former method will modify your original image, while the latter method will open a new window with the thresholded image. The red parts (that is, the above-threshold values) in the original image are now white, while the non-red parts (that is, the below-threshold values) in the original image are now black. Sometimes, the threshold is not perfect and has gaps or holes in places where the signal was not even. You will learn how to deal with these issues in the *Morphological processing* section. The three stages of this process are shown in the following image:

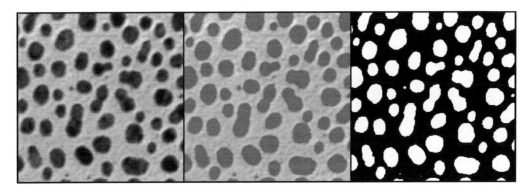

The image in the left panel is the original image. The middle panel shows the auto threshold with the foreground areas in red. The right panel shows the resulting mask that was created based on the threshold.

Thresholding color images

As mentioned earlier, color images are more complicated to segment. When talking about color images, it is important to distinguish between RGB images and multichannel stacks. The latter can be thresholded just fine using the techniques described in the previous section. Multichannel stacks can be seen as individual grayscale images that were given a specific LUT to appear colored. RGB images, on the other hand, are a little more complex. If the image only contains pixels that are red, green, or blue, you could convert the image into a multichannel image.

To segment an RGB image with more colors, you need to transform the image to a different color space. To select the foreground based on color, the HSB color space is more convenient. As we saw in the *Chapter 2, Basic Image Processing with ImageJ,* the color information in HSB images is a separate channel encoded in grayscale values. When you want to set a threshold on an RGB color image in ImageJ and Fiji, the **Threshold Color** dialog opens automatically:

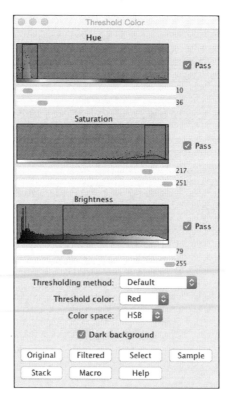

By default, it opens in the HSB color space, where the top chart shows the distribution of the hue channel. The two sliders underneath indicate which colors you wish to select. In this case, orange is selected. The second panel shows the controls for saturation. As the sliders are far to the right, we only select bright orange colors. Finally, the third panel at the bottom shows the controls for brightness, which is set for a wide range of brightness values starting at the mid-level. This example shows you how to select a specific range of colors. In this case, the threshold was set to select the hair of the clown in the **Clown** sample image:

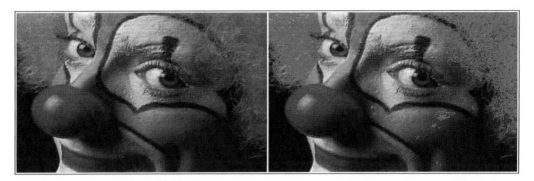

As you can see, the threshold is not perfect. There are small areas on the cheek and near the nose that are also within the threshold. Furthermore, there are also gaps in the area that are part of the hair, especially around the right eye and in the top-right corner of the image.

The threshold method list has the same methods as the standard ImageJ threshold dialog, and it works only on the brightness channel. The **Original** button is similar to the **Reset** option in the grayscale threshold dialog. The **Select** button will convert the thresholded region into a selection. The **Sample** button will use a selected portion of the image to generate a threshold based on the hue, saturation, and brightness channels in that area.

Morphological processing

After segmenting the image into the two components, you are left with a mask or binary image. As was clear from the examples, these masks are not always suitable for direct measurement. Imperfections in the image may result in gaps in objects or small discontinuities in structures. Also, some areas might be detected as foreground when they are actually not really objects of interest. You could manually correct this by converting the missing pixels to white or black in order to include or exclude them, respectively. In some cases, this might be the only possible recourse. However, in many cases, there are a few processing steps available that can fix these problems in a systematic way. These steps are called morphological processing, which we will examine in greater detail in the next section.

Morphological operators

ImageJ supports the two main principal operators for morphological processing: **erode** and **dilate**. It also has functions for filling holes, skeletonizing, and watershedding binary images, which will be discussed in a later section. These functions will be explained in the upcoming sections using a few basic examples.

Erode and dilate

To start with, we will look at the basic operators **erode** and **dilate**. The erode operator takes a foreground pixel (**FG**) and looks at the surrounding pixels in a 3 x 3 neighborhood. Based on the number of FG pixels, the pixel will be changed to a background pixel (**BG**), or it stays as an FG pixel. The dilate operator functions in the opposite way. ImageJ determines whether a pixel will be changed or not based on the binary options, which can be set by going to **Process | Binary | Options...**:

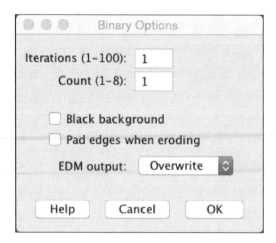

Iterations determines how many times the operator is repeated, and **Count** determines the number of pixels used for the threshold that determines whether a pixel is switched or not. **EDM output** determines where the results from distance mapping functions are written. When **Overwrite** is selected, the distance mapping overwrites the pixels in your mask image. **Pad edges when eroding** determines whether pixels will be eroded when they are located on the edge of the image. When selected, there will be no erosion at the edges of the image.

For the following example, I will assume that the number of iterations is set to 1, the count to 1, and the black background is unchecked.

1. Open the `4909_03b_binary.tif` image in ImageJ. It is available on the Packt website.

2. Set a threshold for the image using 0 for the top slider and 75 for the bottom slider, using the default method. Leave the dark background unchecked.

3. Select **Edit | Selection | Create Mask** to generate a new image or press **Apply** in the threshold dialog to overwrite the original image.

4. Finally, select the masked image and press *Ctrl + Shift + I* to invert the image so that it has a white background. You should now have the following result (the original is on the left-hand side and the mask is on the right-hand side):

Binary processing in ImageJ	Binary processing in ImageJ

When you look closely at the masked image, you will appreciate that there are a few small problems. Most notably, the letter **a** in **Binary** and **ImageJ** is broken in three disconnected parts. Also, the letters **p** and **g** are not entirely complete and have a break but are not completely disconnected. For humans, this is not a large problem. We can easily fill in the gaps in our minds and read the text. Computers, on the other hand, may have a more difficult time trying to decipher the text. We will now look at the effect of binary operators on this mask. You will also see how this may solve our problem of fragmented letters.

1. Select the masked image and go to **Process | Binary | Options...** to open the options dialog. This will show a few more options now that we have a masked image, most notably the **Do** drop-down menu and the **Preview** checkbox.

2. Zoom in on one of the letters a using the magnification tool or the + key on the keyboard.

3. Select **Erode** from the **Do** drop-down menu and check the **Preview** checkbox, but don't press OK!

In preview mode, you will notice that the entire mask went white, and the text completely disappeared when you selected the erode operator. When you increase the value in the **Count** field, you will start to notice that parts of the text will start to come back. With a value of 3, some pixels are visible, while a value of 7 or 8 gives you most of the text unscathed. When the value is set to 8, the only victim of the erode operation is the isolated pixel of the letter **a**. All the other pixels remain intact, but this isolated pixel is removed. This is one of the most used applications of the erode operator — removing isolated single pixels caused by noise in your image.

When using **Erode**, isolated pixels can be removed, but the entire mask becomes smaller, reducing the area that we would like to measure. Using **Dilate** directly after an **Erode** operation (or using **Open**), we can remove isolated pixels while still preserving the area we would like to measure. Once an FG pixel is lost because of **Erode**, it can never return, no matter how many times you use **Dilate**!

Now, select **Dilate** from the **Do** drop-down menu, set **Count** to 1 again, and see what the effect is. When you use the dilate operator, the text will become thicker, but it also fills in the gaps in the letters. This outcome is much more useful. However, there are a few problems here. The bottom tail of the letter **g** as well as the opening of the letter **e** are now filled in. By increasing **Count** to 2, this problem is ameliorated, and the letter **e** as well as the tail of the letter **g** are open again. When **Count** is 2, **Dilate** fixes the problem of the fragments. However, our letters are now much thicker, and some letters have merged. Take a look at **eJ** in the word **ImageJ**. The tail of the letter **e** is directly connected to the tail of the letter **J**. We would now like to take two steps. First, we want to dilate the mask to fill the gaps, and then, we want to erode the mask to get rid of the connected letters. Executing the operators in succession on the mask can perform this combination. First, we will dilate the mask, and then, we will erode the result. However, there is also a special function that performs both steps in this order called **Close**. If you want to perform the steps in the opposite order (first erode and then dilate), you can use the **Open** function.

When you select the **Close** option in the drop-down menu, you can see the result of this action. The result is OK, but not that great. The fact that the result in this case is not that great is caused by the fact that we used different values of **Count** for each step. The **Dilate** operator worked best when we used 2, while the **Erode** operator worked best when we used a value of 7 or 8. For this example, it is better to perform the **Dilate** and **Erode** operators in succession with specific values for count in each step. In the following images, the **Close** operation was used with a value of 2 for count, while the succession of **Dilate** and **Erode** were performed using 2 and 5, respectively (the left-hand-side image is the original mask):

As can be seen in the middle and right panels, both methods have their advantages and drawbacks. The **Close** operation (middle panel) filled in the letter **e**, and there is still an isolated pixel that is part of the letter **a**. However, the letters themselves still have good details. The manual successive dilate/erode steps (right panel) preserved the hole in the letter e as well as the details of the letter **g**. However, the details of the letter **a** are less pronounced. Specifically, the *serif* (the small hook at the bottom-right corner of the letter **a**) is completely lost.

Skeletonize and watershed

After processing the mask using **Dilate**, **Erode**, **Open**, and **Close**, we may want to reduce the mask to the most basic features. The core of the letters that we segmented earlier is formed by the strokes. Each character consists of a set of strokes in different directions, which together define the character. In ImageJ, we can recreate these strokes using the skeletonize function, which can be found by going to **Process | Binary | Skeletonize** in the menu or by selecting it from the **Do** drop-down menu in the binary options dialog. **Skeletonize** looks at each pixel's neighbors and removes a pixel if it is flanked by other FG pixels. This leads to reducing the mask to a single pixel width mask.

When applied to the result of the masks after our close (left panel) and successive dilate/erode (right panel) operations, the results are as follows:

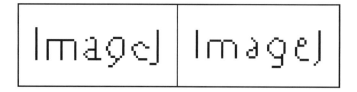

The result from the **Close** operation (left panel) is not very satisfactory. The letter **e** is unrecognizable and looks more like a letter **c**. The successive dilate/erode operation (right panel) has a slightly better result due to the skeletonize operations. Although the letters look a bit funny and wobbly, all the important strokes are present.

The watershed function separates objects that are touching. We will look at the effect of this operation using the blobs sample image. You could apply it to the text example. However, the problem in the text example was the fact that objects needed to be joined not separated.

1. Open the **Blobs** image from the sample images.
2. Set a threshold using the **Default** method, leave the **Dark background** box unchecked, and click on **Apply** to create the mask.
3. Now, go to **Process | Binary | Watershed** from the menu.

The result will look as follows, with the original mask to the left and the result of the watershed operation to the right:

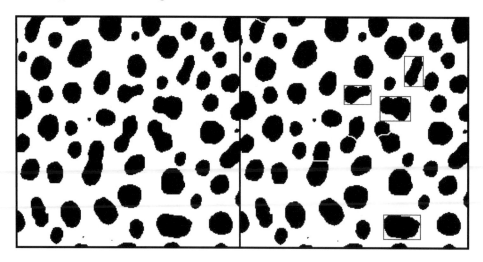

As can be seen, four blobs were split into two separate objects each. This operation looks for areas that are pinched. When an object has a narrow part between two thicker parts (similar to the middle of an 8), it will be separated along the narrow part. Notice, however, that this does not work for some of the blobs (indicated by blue rectangles). When there is no pinch in the outline, the watershed algorithm will not split the object. This would be very useful if you wish to quantify the number of objects when you know that objects can overlap. However, you may run into problems if you wish to measure object size or area. As the overlapping area cannot be measured accurately, the measurements for overlapping objects will underestimate the actual size. This problem can be solved by assuming that the objects have a regular shape, such as an oval, but this might not hold in many cases. In ImageJ, this latter assumption can be used using the particle analyzer, which will be discussed in *Chapter 5, Basic Measurements with ImageJ*. The best way to solve this problem is by making sure that the amount of overlap is reduced, which might require changes in your sample preparation or acquisition.

Image filtering

The previous section looked at ways to segment the image in the foreground and background using a threshold. It also looked at ways to derive a result suitable for analysis with the use of morphological operators. The morphological operators were used to clean the results of the threshold by removing isolated pixels. In most real-life applications, these isolated pixels are due to the effect of noise in your image-acquisition system. Some of the noise can be removed using the techniques described in the previous chapter, but this may not remove all the noise. In this section, we will look at ways to use filters to remove noise and prepare images to create masks. Filtering can be a step that is inserted before thresholding and morphological processing. If your images are high contrast and have extremely low levels of noise, this might not be required. However, this is relatively rare.

There are two categories of filtering, depending on the type of domain that is used for filtering. Images can be seen in two different domains: the **spatial** and the **frequency** domain. The most recognizable to humans is the spatial domain. This is an image as we recognize it from our cameras. Each location in space has a value, and the combination of an area filled with closely spaced locations with differing values forms an image. If all the values were identical, the image would appear uniform as a single color or gray. In the case of digital images, locations are specified by the pixels that form the image, and the value is represented as a gray value or an RGB value.

The frequency domain is less recognizable to humans. An image in the frequency domain is represented by the rate of change of values or frequency. Humans recognize frequency in terms of wavelengths of light. Light with a higher frequency will appear blue/violet, while light with a lower frequency will appear orange/red. However, in image processing, the frequency of an image is determined by the way pixel intensities change within an image, and not necessarily the color of the pixels. I will start with filtering in the frequency domain, as this is more complex. Note that most of the filtering for image processing is done in the spatial domain with excellent results.

Filtering in the frequency domain

Filtering of images is based on a transformation technique described by Joseph Fourier in 1822. This transformation takes data in one domain and transforms it to a different domain and back again. For image processing, the transformation goes from the *spatial domain* to the *frequency domain*. The spatial domain considers points to be in a space, either a plane (2D) or a volume (3D). Each location of a point has an intensity value, which changes over different locations for most images. The rate at which the intensities change along a dimension determines the frequency. Take a look at this artificial image:

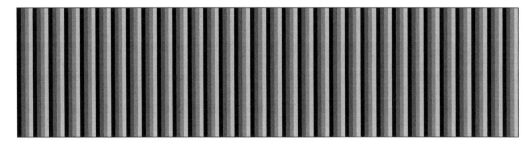

If we look at the profile of intensity along the width of the image as well as along the height of the image in the middle, we would get the following results (horizontal profile to the left and vertical profile to the right):

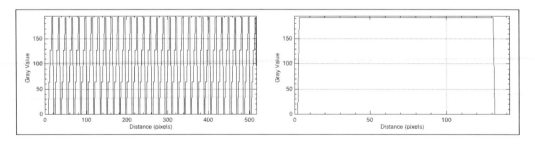

As is obvious from these plots, there is a clear difference in the rate of intensity changes. The horizontal profile (left) shows fast changes in intensity over distance, while the vertical profile (right) shows no change whatsoever. Another way of describing this is that the frequency along the horizontal profile is large, while it is low on the vertical axis.

The Fourier transform will calculate the frequencies in the spatial domain and plot them as frequencies in the X and Y direction. The idea of the transform is based on the fact that any signal can be described as the (infinite) sum of harmonic functions (that is, sines and cosines) with different frequencies. These frequencies are represented by the coefficients for the sines and cosines, which are displayed as gray values by ImageJ in an image. We will obtain the Fourier transform that is, **Fast Fourier Transform (FFT)** of the artificial image by going to **Process | FFT | FFT** from the menu:

The center (that is, origin) of the image has a frequency of 0, while the horizontal line through the origin represents the frequencies along the x axis of the image. The values in the quadrants determine the frequencies along the diagonals of the image. Values close to the center of the image represent low frequencies, while values close to the edge represent higher frequencies. As there is only a change in frequency along the X coordinates of the image, the transformed image shows only vertical lines. If the pattern had been diagonal, the lines in the transformed image would also be diagonal.

The dashed appearance of the lines in the transformed image is caused by the fact that the input image was not square. The width is 512, but the height only 128 pixels. If the image were a 512 x 512 square, the transformed image would only show a row of dots along the x axis through the origin. If you halved the height of the sample image, the dashes become roughly twice as long.

When we use the FFT image as input, we can create the original image when we select **Process | FFT | Inverse FFT** from the menu:

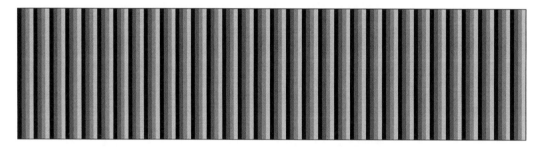

Note that since we used the FFT and immediately the inversed FFT, we actually did not apply any filtering. The image before and after the transform is identical. This is a very desirable feature of the transform, because this means that the transform is lossless. No information was lost during the process. To actually filter the image, we need to modify the transformed image by modifying the pixel values in the transformed image.

To apply some (crude) filtering, we will take the following steps:

1. Select the transformed image.
2. Go to **Edit | Selection | Specify...** from the menu and enter the following values: **Width** as 255, **Height** as 255, **X coordinate** as 0, and **Y coordinate** as 0. Then, press **OK**.
3. Open the color picker by going to **Image | Color | Color Picker** from the menu or pressing *Ctrl + Shift + K* on the keyboard.
4. Make sure that the foreground is set to black by clicking on the little icon of a black-and-white square in the bottom-right corner of the color picker.
5. Now, fill the selection that we specified with black by going to **Edit | Fill** or by pressing *Ctrl + F*.
6. Repeat steps 2 and 5, but now, specify the selection to have the *X* and *Y* coordinates of 257.
7. Finally, go to **Process | FFT | Inverse FFT** from the menu to generate the filtered image.

If you followed the instructions, your FFT image would look as follows:

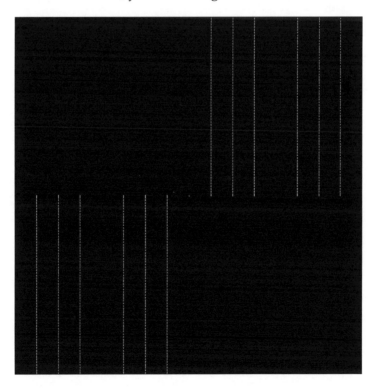

The inverse FFT image will look as follows:

As can be seen in the inverse FFT image, there are now significant differences before and after the manipulations. For instance, the frequency in the vertical direction is different. Each bar now changes intensity as you go from top to bottom. Try the same routine, but this time, specify the selection using the following parameters in step 2, and skip step 6:

- **Width**: 64
- **Height**: 512
- **X coordinate**: 272
- **Y coordinate**: 0

After filling in the selection with black and calculating the inverse FFT, the image will appear as shown here in the right panel. You have specifically removed a small subset of the frequencies from the frequency domain. After calculating the inverse FFT, you will get the following result (zoomed area in the top-left corner):

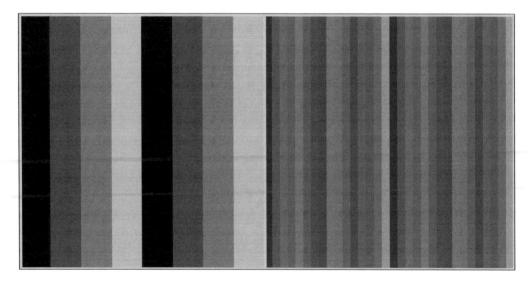

On the left-hand side, you see the original image, and on the right-hand side is the filtered image. As the region selected and removed entailed the lower frequencies, the higher frequencies remain resulting in a greater change in the intensity values along the horizontal axis.

As this example is very artificial, the results here are not necessarily practical for analysis. However, if you have an image that is corrupted by high-frequency intensity changes (for example, imaging noise), you know you have to remove the frequencies at the edge of the FFT transform. On the other hand, if you have a slow gradient of intensity changes (for example, uneven illumination), you need to remove the low frequencies in the FFT transform. Using black to remove the frequencies, you're creating a filter that excludes the frequencies covered by your selection. If you filled the selection with white, you would include all the selected frequencies covered by your selection. In the next section, we will look at filtering in the spatial domain, which is slightly more intuitive to apply.

Image filtering in the spatial domain

Filtering in the spatial domain involves using a filter, usually referred to as a **kernel**. This filter transforms every pixel using a method called **convolution**. Convolution involves taking a center pixel with a small array of neighboring pixels (usually 3 x 3) and multiplying the intensities with a set of weights as defined in the kernel. The sum of the multiplications will become the new pixel intensity for the center pixel. In the following example, there is a part of an image (left), the kernel (middle), and the outcome of the convolution (right):

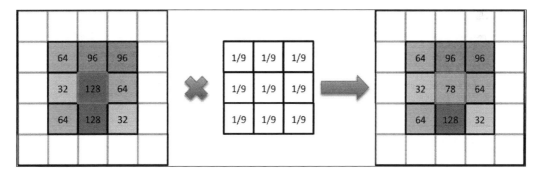

The center pixel (highlighted in orange) and the surrounding pixels in a 3 x 3 neighborhood are multiplied with the kernel (middle). The result of the convolution is shown on the right-hand side. The value of the center pixel used to be 128, but is now 78 after convolution. The kernel shown in this example is a simple smoothing filter (also called a **box** filter). The main effect of this filter is that it averages pixels, resulting in a blurring of the image. The following image is a detail from the **Boats** sample image, before (left) and after (right) convolving with the box filter:

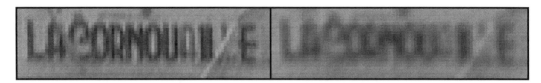

When you change the filter size to 7 x 7, the effect of the smoothing will be much stronger, as more pixels in the neighborhood will influence the value of the center pixel. When using the box filter with a size of 7 x 7, each weight will be equal to 1/49. The result for the same image will look as follows:

Notice that the filtering has almost completely smoothed the letters, making them unrecognizable. The box filter functions as a low-pass filter—only low frequencies in the image will remain. This is caused by the fact that fast changes in intensity will be smoothed out more aggressively by the box filter than the low frequencies. Even though this filtering happens in the spatial domain, the effects are also reflected in the frequency domain.

To recreate the preceding images, follow these steps on the **Boats** image from the sample images:

1. Select **Process | Filters | Convolve...** from the menu and remove everything in the text field in the dialog that opens.

2. Type three 1s separated by a space and press enter. Repeat this twice.

3. Make sure that the **Normalize kernel** checkbox is selected and press **OK**.

4. The image now looks a little less sharp as it has been convolved with a 3 x 3 box filter.

If you want to convolve with a 7 x 7 box filter, just type seven rows of seven 1s separated by spaces, and repeat the steps on a newly opened Boats image to see the effect of kernel size.

 When applying the kernel on an image that was already convolved, the effect will be larger than when the image wasn't convolved yet. When using the 3 x 3 box filter twice in succession, the effect will be the same as running a 3 x 3 box filter with weights of 1/81 per pixel (*1/9 * 1/9*).

The result of filtering using a kernel depends on the values of the weights that you specify and the kernel's size. Typically, there are two types of kernel that can be separated based on the sum of their weights. When the sum of the weights in a kernel adds up to 1, the kernel is called normalized. The advantage of a normalized kernel is that the result of the convolution will not exceed the maximum pixel value allowed by the bit depth of the image. When the **Normalized kernel** checkbox is checked in the **Convolve** dialog, ImageJ will automatically take care of the normalization. Non-normalized kernels can exhibit clamping artifacts. When the sum of the kernel exceeds 1, the result of convolution may exceed the maximum allowable value (that is, 255 for 8-bit images). When this happens, the value after the transformation will be clamped at the maximum value. This clamping may result in artifacts such as blocks of white pixels.

The box filter is a very simple filter, but it does not discriminate any features in the image. It averages evenly in all directions. Other filters exist that actually enhance certain features in your image. An example of such a filter is the **Mexican hat** filter. This filter emphasizes the center pixel over the surrounding pixels:

0	0	-1	0	0
0	-1	-2	-1	0
-1	-2	16	-2	-1
0	-1	-2	-1	0
0	0	-1	0	0

The Mexican hat filter is shaped a little like a sombrero, hence the name. It makes areas with high contrast become bright, while areas of uniform intensity become darker. Applied on the **Boats** image, the result looks as follows:

What stands out immediately is the fact that the edges of the letters are greatly emphasized. This makes sense because the contrast is relatively strong. These are black letters on a mostly even light-gray background. The only edges that are not clearly recognizable are the points where the letters touch each other and the places where the ropes hide parts of the letters. You can imagine that this filter might also work well for the text example and the segmentation of the blobs mentioned earlier. It basically functions as a high-pass filter. Only regions with fast changes in intensity are emphasized, while regions with slow changes in intensity (that is, low frequencies) are reduced.

Besides entering kernel weights manually, ImageJ and Fiji also have some common filter kernels that can be accessed by going to **Process | Filters**. Two of the most often used filter kernels include the **Gaussian Blur...** and the **Mean...** filter. The latter is identical to the box filter. The former is similar to the Mexican hat filter. However, it does not use negative values in the kernel. The **Gaussian Blur** filter smoothens the image just like a box filter does, but it does it in a more gradual way. The advantage of **Gaussian Blur** is that it can have fewer artifacts when you apply it. The response of the filter in the frequency domain is also better, making it possible to combine spatial and frequency domain filtering.

Next, we will look at some operators that can be used to detect specific features in an image that may be relevant for processing. These operators also use convolution, but they have different properties compared to the filters described earlier.

Feature extraction

As we saw in the earlier sections, filters can be used to isolate different frequencies using filters. By convolving an image with a Mexican hat filter, high frequencies are preserved, while using the box filter has the opposite effect. The difference between the filters in this section and the filters in the previous section is in specificity. The Mexican hat filter had no preference for direction. When there was an edge with sharp contrast (quick change in intensity), the filter had a strong effect. However, sometimes, you are only interested in a specific type of edge. Let's assume that we only want to detect vertical edges. The Mexican hat filter will give us all the edges in all directions, not just the vertical ones. This will be the topic of the following section.

Edge detection

To detect only vertical edges, we need to create a kernel that emphasizes pixels that are in a vertical orientation. The following kernels can detect different orientations of edges:

	vertical			horizontal		
Prewitt	-1	0	1	-1	-1	-1
	-1	0	1	0	0	0
	-1	0	1	1	1	1
Sobel	-1	0	1	-1	-2	-1
	-2	0	2	0	0	0
	-1	0	1	-1	-2	-1

To perform the **Sobel edge** detection, you can use the **Find Edges** command from the **Process** menu. This command will run both the horizontal and the vertical Sobel kernel over the image.

Finally, there is also the **Canny procedure** for edge detection that involves five steps. This procedure was developed by John F. Canny and consists of the following steps:

1. Apply Gaussian smoothing to remove noise.
2. Detect gradients in the image using edge detection.
3. Thin edges using convolution with a kernel such as the Mexican hat.
4. Apply two different thresholds to determine weak and strong edges.
5. Remove weak edges that are not connected to strong edges.

The first three steps involve using different kernels for smoothing, edge detection, and edge thinning in succession. Note that the first step is only required if the image is degraded by noise. If the contrast is high and noise is absent, this step can be skipped. This step is also the weakest point of the procedure. Both noise and edges are forms of high-frequency signals, and the Gaussian filter smoothens both equally. If noise is present, techniques that reduce the noise specifically while leaving the edges intact should show great improvement.

Summary

In this chapter, we looked at ways to separate an image into foreground and background. We saw different methods to set the threshold in grayscale and color images. We applied filtering in the spatial and frequency domains to aid in cleaning the image and extracting edges for further processing. All these steps will help us when we wish to measure objects in the image, which is the topic of the next chapter.

5

Basic Measurements with ImageJ

We saw in the previous chapter how to perform some preprocessing steps that prepared the image data for measurement and analysis. In this chapter, we will take a closer look at the measurement system available in ImageJ. You will also learn how to create some visualizations of movement and dynamics. We will look at the following topics in this chapter:

- Selections and regions
- The ROI Manager
- Kymographs and line profiles
- Area and line selections
- Semiquantitative colocalization
- Particle analysis

Selections and regions in ImageJ

We will first look at the tools that are available in ImageJ to select **Regions Of Interest (ROIs)**. These tools can be useful if you wish to only process a small portion of your image. ROIs are a very important element in ImageJ, and there is also a specific manager to handle the ROIs: **ROI Manager**. It can be opened by going to **Analyze | Tools | ROI Manager...**, which will open the following window:

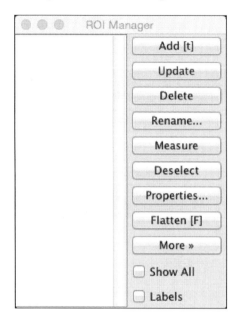

On the left-hand side, there is a list that will contain the ROIs, while on the right-hand side, there are several buttons that will perform certain actions on the ROIs. The checkboxes in the bottom-right corner allow the user to see all the regions at once (**Show All**), while the **Labels** checkbox displays the region label in the image.

There are different types of region that are supported by ImageJ. They can be divided into two major types: **area selections** and **line selections**. A third singular type is the **Point ROI**, which only has one member. When used for measurements, the parameters that can be measured are slightly different. Area can only be measured with the area type ROIs, while angle can only be measured with line selections.

First, I will discuss a few of the common selection types that are supported by ImageJ, and then, we will apply them to take measurements.

Area selections

Area selections in ImageJ contain different types with different properties. The following types are available in ImageJ:

- Rectangles
- Ovals
- Polygons
- Freehand

Rectangles are mostly used to select areas to crop images or for rectangular objects. If your images contain more organic shapes, oval or polygon areas are more suitable. These types can be added to images by selecting the appropriate tool in the toolbar of the ImageJ program. Then, you can left-click and drag the mouse to enclose the area you wish to select and then release the mouse button. After the selection has been set, you can press the **Add** button on the ROI Manager (or press *Ctrl + T*) to add the region to the ROI Manager.

If the **Require control/command key for shortcuts** option is unchecked when you go to **Edit | Options | Misc...**, then pressing only the letter *T* is sufficient to add the ROI to the Manager.

When an ROI is added to the ROI Manager, it can be saved to a file to preserve it for later. When multiple ROIs are added to the ROI Manager and one is selected when attempting to save the ROIs, only the selected ROI will be saved. If you wish to save all the ROIs at once, press **Deselect** to unselect all ROIs. Alternatively, you can use *Ctrl + A* to select all the ROIs, before selecting **More » | Save** from the ROI Manager.

Single ROIs will be saved to the disk as a file with the .roi extension. Multiple ROIs will be saved as an ROI set in a .zip file. This zip archive contains individual .roi files, one for each selection. On Windows, extensions are hidden by default for known file types. So, to see the extensions, you may have to uncheck the **Hide extensions for known file types** option in the folder options.

When adding additional ROIs, it may be convenient to select the **Show All** checkbox in the ROI Manager. This will show all the ROIs currently in the list. Clicking on the ROI in the ROI Manager can set the active region. It always shows in the color you have set in the options (refer to, *Chapter 1, Getting Started with ImageJ*), with small white squares at the corners:

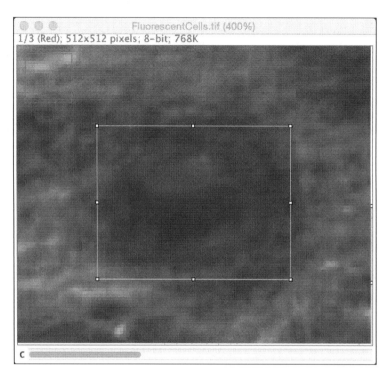

These small squares are control points that can be used to move and resize the ROI. If you modify a region by resizing it or positioning it, pressing the **Update** button on the ROI Manager will update the region in the list. To resize, click and drag one of the squares to a new location and release the mouse button. If you hold the *Shift* key while dragging the handles, the shape will become a square or circle with equal width and height. If you hold the *Ctrl* key (or *Cmd* key on a Mac) while clicking on the control points, the region grows in width and height equally around the center. If you hold the *Alt* key while resizing, the handle on the opposite side will stay at a fixed location while you resize the region, keeping the length-to-width proportion equal. If you press the *Alt* key and create an area that overlaps with your previous region, a subtraction of the overlapping part of the two regions will be formed. Conversely, if you hold the *Shift* key before creating a new region that overlaps a previous region, you will create a union of the overlapping part of the two regions:

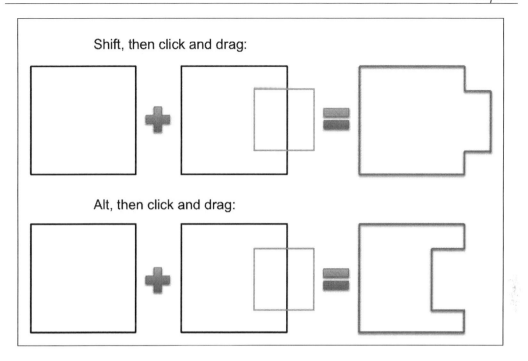

A combination of two of the keys can also be pressed while dragging for a combination of both resizing effects. To move a region, move the cursor inside the region and click and drag the region to a new location. Make sure that the cursor is shaped like an arrow—and not like a hand or crosshair—before you click and drag the region. For small regions, you might have to zoom in in order to move the region. If the cursor gets close to the control points, it will change to resize mode.

Once a region is placed and added to the ROI Manager, pushing the **Measure** button in the ROI Manager or using the *Ctrl + M* keyboard shortcut will measure the region. To select the parameters that are measured, go to **Analyze | Set Measurements...** to select the parameters:

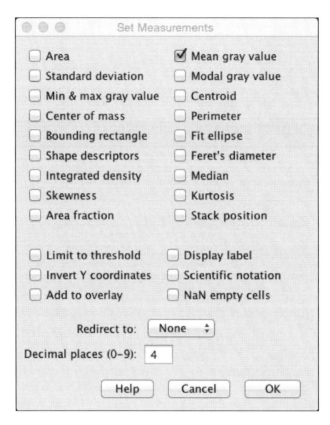

Mean gray value is the average intensity within the area, while **Area** measures the area of the region in the units of the image. Once you click on **Measure** in the ROI Manager, a new window with the measurements is opened. This window shows the results. Some of the different measurements will be explained in the *Area selections and measurements* section, where we will use them to extract useful information from our images.

Line selections

The line selections contain the following types:

- Straight line
- Segmented line
- Angle tool

ImageJ handles these selection types in a similar way. However, they can be used for different measurements. One of the most used functions for line segments is to plot a profile along a line or segmented line. Another option is to create a **kymograph**. Both these options will be demonstrated in the upcoming sections.

Point selections

The third type of selection only contains one tool: the point tool. It selects a single pixel only and is mostly used in counting or marking an object's center point. The advantage of point selection is that it requires only a single click to place it. However, the measurements that can be obtained are limited to the X and Y coordinates and the intensity.

Basic measurements

We will now look at a few techniques that can be used to measure specific parameters from data. For these measurements, we will use the ROI Manager and several different types of region to select and measure intensities, speed, and other interesting things. Besides measurements, regions can also be used for other purposes relevant to processing and image handling. One useful application of selections is that they can be used to limit certain processing steps to the selected area while leaving the unselected pixels unaffected. A few examples of these applications will be demonstrated as well.

Area selections and measurements

We will start with some basic measurements using area selections. We will use these to measure some basic parameters such as area, perimeter (or circumference), and many more. We will start with the most basic area selection: the rectangle.

Rectangular selections are very useful for cropping image areas. By reducing the size of an image, you reduce the memory required as well as the processing time for complicated algorithms. Another good use for a rectangular selection is to restrict processing in a larger image to a specific region. Some ImageJ algorithms and tools can work within an active selection. We will see an example of this type of application in a plugin that we will develop in *Chapter 9, Creating ImageJ Plugins for Analysis*. As a result of the simplicity of the rectangle, measurements, such as area and perimeter are not really relevant. You can calculate the area and perimeter of a rectangle very easily using the width and height. We will, therefore, focus on some more useful applications of rectangular selections.

To start with, let's use the rectangular selection to modify a small section of an image by inverting its gray values. To start with an example, open the **Blobs** image from the sample images. We will invert the LUT for a single blob using these steps:

1. Select a blob in the image using the rectangular selection tool.

2. After selecting a blob, press *Ctrl + Shift + I* to invert the LUT.

3. Use *Ctrl + Shift + A* to remove all selections and invert the LUT again using *Ctrl + Shift + I*.

In this little exercise, we focused on only modifying pixels that were selected, while the pixels outside of the selection were left unchanged. If no pixels were selected, the **Invert LUT** command worked on all pixels. This is an example of how to use area selection to limit processing to selected pixels only. The same method also works for other area selections. You could also use this method to highlight a specific part of an image by making it stand out. For instance, in the following kymograph example, we could show the lines that were acquired during stimulation by creating a square selection and inverting the LUT for only that time period.

Oval selections

ImageJ has two types of selection for rounded shapes: **ellipses** and **ovals**. The difference between the two types is subtle, but oval selections can only by shaped along the x or y axis. Ellipses, on the other hand, can be freely rotated as well. To create a circle, hold the *Shift* key while creating an oval selection to force ImageJ to make a circle with equal width and height. Another important property of oval selections is their shape descriptors. The shape descriptors that ImageJ reports in its measurements are the circularity (Circ.), roundness (Round), aspect ratio (AR), and solidity (Solidity). Circularity is defined as follows:

$$Circ. = 4\pi \cdot \frac{A}{C^2}$$

Here, *A* is the area, and *C* is the circumference. Roundness is defined as follows:

$$Round = 4 \cdot \frac{A}{\pi \cdot [Major\ Axis]^2}$$

Here, the major axis is the largest diameter of an oval. Aspect ratio is the ratio between the major and minor axes of an oval. Solidity is defined as the area divided by the convex hull of the area. Solidity is helpful for irregular shapes. A convex hull is the smallest curve that can be fitted around an object without intersecting with it. It can be seen as trying to stretch an elastic band around the object to encompass it completely. For oval- or ellipse-shaped objects, this parameter does not add any information.

Let's look at some of the results when drawing a few ellipses and ovals and measuring their shape descriptors. Here are a few examples of elliptical selections (left of the image) and oval selections (right of the image):

The shapes with a circularity of 1.00 are colored orange (ellipse) and light green (oval). The red ellipse has a very low circularity (0.28), while the cyan oval has an intermediate circularity (0.48). This circularity parameter will be useful when trying to detect particles, as it is a very basic description of a shape using a single value. Round objects will have a value of 1, while flattened ovals will have a low value closer to 0.

It is also possible to create a doughnut selection using the oval tool. Making two circles, one bigger than the other, and then removing the smaller of the two circles can do this. The following steps will create a doughnut selection:

1. Create the larger circle first over the object you wish to select and press *Ctrl + T* to add it to the ROI Manager. Make the size of the circle 20 x 20 pixels.

2. To create the inner circle, you can add a new circle using the oval tool. However, it may not be centered. To create a centered inner circle, we will select the outer circle and select **Edit | Selection | Enlarge…** from the menu.

3. Enter a value of -5 to shrink the circle to a new circle of 10 x 10 pixels and press *Ctrl + T* to add it to the ROI Manager.

4. To create the doughnut, select both circles in the ROI Manager.

5. With both circles selected, select **More » | XOR** from the ROI Manager. This will result in the doughnut. To add the new selection, press *Ctrl + T*.

Note that creating a doughnut this way forces the new area selection to be "pixelated". The outline of the region will be aligned across the pixel grid unlike the ROIs generated by ImageJ. You can also create the doughnut by holding the *Alt* key while creating the inner circle. However, it can be difficult to align both circles properly.

Polygon selections

Other types of area selection are polygon and freehand selections. They allow more organic shapes to be selected. To create a polygon selection, select the tool and by left-clicking, you can add points to the polygon. Each point is connected by a straight line (vertex), and by double-clicking or by left-clicking on the first point, the polygon is closed and turns into an area selection. If you right-click, the polygon tool will add a point at the point where you clicked and close the polygon at the same time. A polygon requires a minimum of three points. This is tool is helpful for selecting irregular shapes, such as in the **Blobs** example:

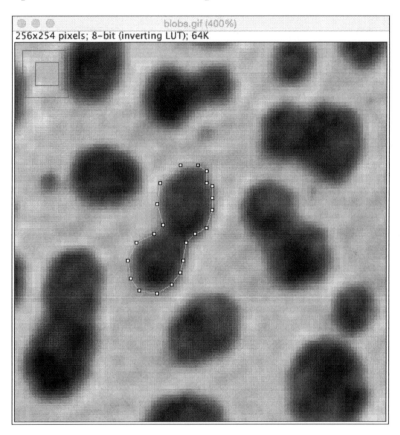

For this type of irregular shape, the polygon tool is more suited to only selecting the blob. A similar effect can be achieved with the freehand tool. However, it may be more difficult to select very precisely. The freehand tool works by left-clicking and holding the button while you drag the mouse around the shape.

Another way of creating an irregular area selection is to use the magic wand selection tool. This tool works in the same way as the wand tool in other graphics programs such as Photoshop and Gimp. It selects pixels that have the same intensity or color as the one that was clicked. To select a blob in the sample image, we can follow these steps:

1. Select the **Wand Tool** from the toolbar.

2. Left-click on a blob. This will create a selection.

3. Change the tolerance for the selection by double-clicking on the wand tool button and set **Tolerance** to 60. Then, press **OK** (see the following screenshot).

4. Left-click on the same blob to see the effect of the tolerance setting on the selection:

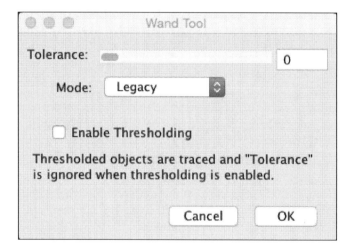

The wand tool allows us to set a tolerance, which means that values that fall within the tolerance relative to the selected pixel will be included in the selection. A value of 0 will only consider pixels that are identical. When enabling thresholding, the tolerance will be ignored (basically, it is set to 0). The mode allows you to use the 4-connected or 8-connected neighbors to determine the selection. The difference between a tolerance of 0 (left image) and 60 (right image) for the blobs example can be as follows:

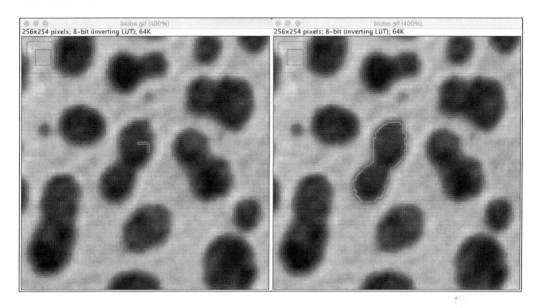

This tool can be very efficient for selecting organic shapes such as these blobs. However, it requires the contrast between the object (the blobs) and the background to be high. If you set the tolerance higher, in the blobs example for instance, not only is the object selected, but also background. If you try a tolerance value of 150 in the blobs example, the selection would still be OK. However, it already includes some background pixels. A tolerance value of 160, however, would include almost the entire image if you click on one of the blobs' lighter pixels. There is a different way to select organic shapes such as blobs using the particle analyzer, which will be discussed later on.

Line selections and measurements

Besides the area selection tools for measurements, there are also line selection tools that can be used for measurements. Line selections can be useful to select thin, elongated structures. Brain cells have a basic structure with a cell body and long, thin processes called **neurites**. Measuring along these thin processes can be done using line selections to determine characteristics such as length. In time series, a line along the neurite will allow for measurement of intensity over time using a specialized visualization of dynamics called a kymograph.

Kymographs

A kymograph is a representation of all the pixels along a line for each frame or slice. This type of image shows the dynamics of objects. Straight lines that run from top to bottom of the image represent static objects, while angled lines indicate movement. The steeper the angle, the faster the object moves. This can be used to measure the velocity of objects. It is also a very simple visual aid to identify movement in a confined space. This latter point is an important distinction. Any object that starts on the line but leaves it on either side will not be visualized and cannot be measured.

Let's look at a very basic kymograph of the time series we used in the previous chapter when we normalized a time series. Open the `time_series.tif` image in ImageJ. Next, we will trace one of the stretches where many puncta are present. To trace an irregular shape like we have here, we want to select the segmented line region.

1. Right-click on the line tool in the ImageJ main interface and select **Segmented Line** from the options presented.

2. Draw a line as indicated in the following image (feel free to take a different stretch).

3. If you wish to create multiple kymographs, you can add each line to the ROI manager using *Ctrl + T*.

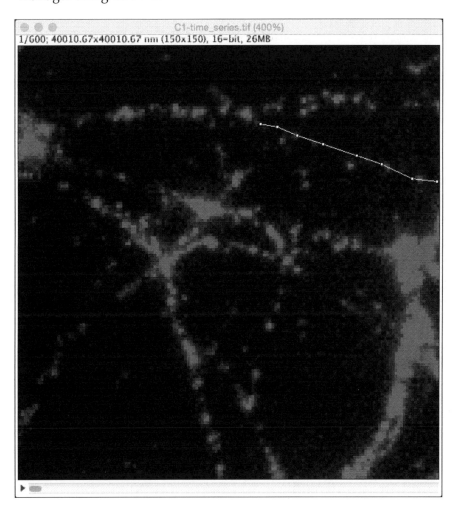

Make sure that the line that you draw intersects the puncta and that you stay along their path. As stated earlier, the kymograph will only show what is on the line! As an exercise, you can draw a line more accurately by first creating a maximum projection and drawing the line there and then transferring it to the time series. To do so, perform the following steps:

1. Create a maximum projection by going to **Image | Stacks | Z Project...** and selecting **Maximum intensity**.

2. In the new image, select a stretch using the segmented line and add it to the ROI Manager.

3. Select the original `time_series.tif` window.

4. Transfer the selection by either selecting the added ROI from the ROI Manager or by going to **Edit | Selection | Restore Selection** from the menu. Note that the latter option will only work for the last active selection, while the former option will work for any number of selections.

Now that we have our line, we will create the kymograph by going to **Image | Stacks | Reslice [/]...** from the menu. Alternatively, you can press the forward slash key (/). If you have a recent version of Fiji, you could also select **Analyze | Multi Kymograph | Multi Kymograph** to create a kymograph. When using the **Reslice** option, follow these steps:

1. Make sure that the line is the active selection by selecting it in the ROI Manager.

2. Select **Image | Stacks | Reslice** from the menu or press the forward slash key.

3. Select the **Avoid interpolation** checkbox and press **OK**.

After pressing **OK**, a new image opens. It has a width equal to the length of the line and a height equal to the number of frames (600). Here are the first 300 lines from the earlier selection:

When using Fiji, using the **Multi Kymograph** tool that is located in the **Analyze** menu can generate the same effect. This plugin has an additional feature that allows you to average a few pixels along the line's length. This will reduce the effects of noise along the line by averaging pixel intensities. To use this plugin, use these steps:

1. Select line selection in the ROI Manager.
2. Select **Analyze | Multi Kymograph | Multi Kymograph** from the menu.
3. Enter a value for line thickness: a value larger than 1 will create an average, in this case use 3 and press **OK**.

The kymograph clearly shows that some of the puncta are moving, while others are more static. Depending on the line you drew, you should get more or less the same result, although some areas have less movement. As this selection was a single line, it is also clear from this example that some of the puncta move in a different direction than others.

To measure velocity in a kymograph (remember that velocity is distance divided by time), all we have to do is draw a single line across each section that is not vertical. Vertical lines have zero distance and, therefore, a velocity of 0. To make it a little easier to do the calculations, we will first change the calibration of the image (refer to *Chapter 2, Basic Image Processing with ImageJ,* for details on how to do this). Set the pixel width to `266.67` and the pixel height to `0.125`. The unit can be set to pixel. What we do here is specify that the width (*x* coordinates) is in nanometers, while the height (*y* coordinates) is in seconds. ImageJ does not fully support this notion, but this will function for our purposes nonetheless.

To perform the measurement, proceed as follows:

1. Select the **Straight Line** tool and draw a line through the center of a track for as long as the line stays in the middle of that track.

2. Make sure that the **Bounding box** option is selected in your measurements.

3. Press *Ctrl + M* to measure the current selection, which will be added to your results.

4. Measure the next part of the track by dragging the top handle of your line to the next point where the track starts to change velocity and measure again.

5. Repeat this process until the track disappears from the kymograph.

As the **Bounding box** option was selected, you will have four columns in your results table, labeled **BX**, **BY**, **Width**, and **Height**. For velocity measurements, we only require the width and height parameters. The width is equal to the distance that was traveled, while the height is equal to the time spent traveling. To get the correct value for velocity, we will divide the width by the height to get the velocity, expressed in *nm/sec* with the calibration mentioned earlier.

This method of calculating the velocity for moving particles is not very difficult, but it is very time consuming and error prone. Also, kymographs are not suited for objects that travel in arbitrary directions in space (that is, not along a line). So, for that type of object and for a more detailed approach to tracking the movement of objects, we will revisit this topic in a later chapter.

Line profiles

In the previous section, we saw what we can do using a simple line selection and a time series for quantification. Line selections can also be used for single images, especially when quantifying features related to intensity, (co) localization, and intactness. For these types of assessment, we would like to know the intensity profile of an object. To create an intensity profile, we can use a straight line or a segmented line selection.

In the following example, we will look at the distribution of rings within a section of a tree. When trees grow, they add a ring every year of young wood. The thicker a ring is, the faster the tree grows, indicating favorable conditions for growth (sunlight, mild temperatures, rainfall, soil conditions, and so on). For this kind of analysis, we need to know two things: the number of rings and the thickness of each ring.

To start with, open the **Tree Rings** image from **File | Open Samples**. The image that opens shows a partial section of a tree, with the tree center at location (135,54), approximately. The rings can be seen as white areas separated by dark lines. Each dark line is the boundary of a growth ring. When you zoom in on the center of the tree, it is immediately apparent that the rings are not equal in width. The fourth ring, for instance, is quite thin, while the fifth ring is five times thicker. For the analysis, we could use the same strategy that we used for the kymograph. We could draw a line from dark border to border and measure the length each time. This has a very big drawback. It is very time consuming (again), and it will be difficult to keep the line straight. Measuring the width of each ring should be based on the shortest distance between each ring border.

To create a line profile, select a line across a section of the image that you wish to profile and go to **Analyze | Plot Profile** from the menu (or press *Ctrl + K*):

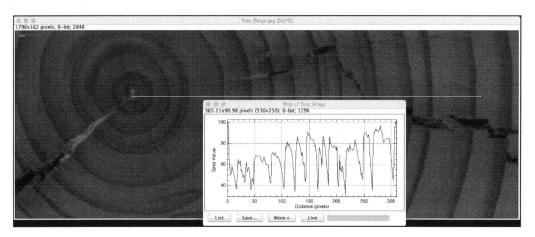

This shows the line profile at the bottom of the figure across the line in the image. It shows the intensity along the line's pixels. The plot profile window also has an option to show a live updating plot. This means that when the region is moved or resized, the plot is updated immediately. Each of the low points in the profile indicates a tree ring border. When we press the **List** button in the **Plot Profile** window, a window opens with intensity values for each pixel along the line. If we copy this to a spreadsheet program, we can calculate the distance between each valley to determine the width of each ring in pixels (without calibrating the image, the real width in practical units is unknown). The number of valleys gives the number of years.

Alternatively, it is possible to measure the widths of the rings using the profile plot as shown earlier. To do this, we must draw a segmented line on the profile plot. Every graphics window (text and results windows excluded) in ImageJ can be used to draw selections. For this example, it is important to disable grid lines in the profile plot before creating the profile plot. This can be done by unchecking the **Draw grid lines** checkbox in the profile plot settings, which can be found by selecting **Edit | Options | Profile Plot Options...** from the menu.

1. Draw a segmented line from the lowest point of each valley starting from the left-hand side.

2. Set the foreground color to black using the color picker and draw the line using *Ctrl + D* or by going to **Edit | Draw** from the menu.

3. Make sure that your measurement settings include the **Bounding rectangle** option.

4. Select the wand tool to measure the area underneath the graph. To measure the width of a tree ring, click with the wand tool above your segmented line, but below the black line of the graph. This will select the white pixels of the chart, which is continuous up to the black line of the graph. You will see that only the section underneath the graph until your segmented line selection is selected (see the following image).

5. When you press *Ctrl + M* to measure this selection, you will get the width and height for the selection.

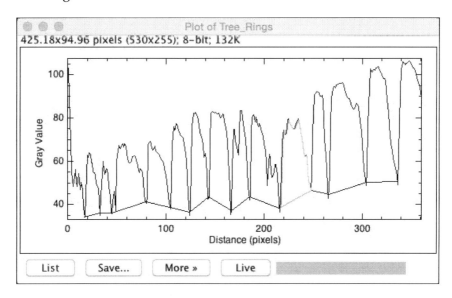

The width measurement will be the thickness of the tree ring. By doing this for each area between the valleys, you can measure the thickness of each ring. Note that if the area underneath the graph is meaningful for your measurements, then selecting **Area** in your measurement options would give you this parameter as well. A similar method is used when analyzing electrophoresis gels and western blots. For this purpose, ImageJ has a special collection of tools to analyze gels. These tools can be found by going to **Analyze | Gels**, with an explanation of how to use it at `http://imagej.nih.gov/ij/docs/guide/146-30.html#toc-Subsection-30.13` and a video explaining it at `http://imagejdocu.tudor.lu/doku.php?id=video:analysis:gel_quantification_analysis`.

Colocalization

In the previous sections, we looked at ways to measure certain aspects of our images, such as velocity and length. This section will look at a different aspect of measurements that involve the colocalization of different signals. Colocalization means that two (or more) objects are within proximity of each other. Whenever two signals overlap in space, we can conclude that they are at the same location, within the boundaries of the resolution that an imaging system allows us. In biology, the localization of two labeled structures or proteins provides clues to whether the protein is contained within a structure or whether it moves to a certain location after being stimulated. For dynamic structures such as cells, we can observe a change in the amount of colocalization, depending on time or stimulation.

Semiquantitative colocalization

Semiquantitative colocalization means that you examine the amount of colocalization by eye or using a crude measurement and classify it (rather arbitrarily) as colocalized or not. This can be a very good place to start off. However, it is very difficult to conclude anything if the results are not black and white. For this type of colocalization, we only require an image for each signal, and we need to merge them to see the colocalization. This is sometimes done automatically when we acquire images, and sometimes, images need to be merged by hand. To merge two different images, a few prerequisites need to be met:

- Images need to be the same size (X, Y, and optionally Z or T)
- Images need to be the same type (8-bit, 16-bit, and so on)
- Images cannot be moved between each channel's acquisition

If these conditions are met, then the result of the colocalization should provide a qualitative result.

To merge two channels, go to **Image | Color | Merge Channels...** from the menu. Currently, ImageJ supports merging seven different images into a single multichannel image using seven different LUTs: red, green, blue, gray, cyan, magenta, and yellow. The most frequently used combination is **Red/Green**, where colocalization results in yellow pixels. Another good combination of colors is **Green/Magenta**, with colocalization showing as white pixels. The latter option is recommended for publications, as people with color-blindness can still appreciate the colocalization. Note that if one channel has very low intensities and the other channel has high intensities, the human visual system will only perceive the brighter channel. For a good visualization of colocalization, both channels need a similar distribution of gray values. The respective histograms should look similar.

A simple way to quantify this colocalization in a rudimentary way is to look at the overlap of bright pixels. To do this, we can take a threshold for each channel and create a mask for each image. To look at the overlap, we can use the image calculator to perform an AND operation. Overlap of pixels is classified as pixels that are 1 (technically, 255) at the same location in both images. After performing this AND operation, we can determine the amount of overlap by counting the number of white pixels in the resulting image. A simple way to do this is by taking the histogram by pressing *Ctrl + H* and then pressing the **List** button in the resulting histogram window. By looking at the value for 255 (at the bottom of the list), you will get a count for the number of pixels that overlap. We will revisit this topic in *Chapter 8, Anatomy of ImageJ Plugins*, where we will apply more rigorous quantification using some of the plugins supplied with Fiji.

Particle analysis

This section will look at the methods available for particle analysis, a field that deals with detecting multiple (similar) objects within an image, with the purpose of segmenting and quantifying them. Many problems can be defined as a particle system, which consists of many individual cells within a single image, holes in a surface, detecting cars on a road, and so on. The basic particle analysis step is detecting or segmenting the particles in a single image.

Preprocessing and preparations

To detect particles, they first need to be separated from the background. To do this, we need to create a mask that isolates all the objects from the background. We already saw how to set a threshold in the previous chapter and how to use it to create a mask. This mask image will be used for particle analysis. For this example, we will use a relatively simple example. Open the **Blobs** image by going to **File | Open Samples** in the ImageJ menu. When the image opens, go to **Image | Adjust | Threshold...** and set the threshold using the **Auto** button. Make sure that **Dark background** box is not checked. You should now see something similar to the following image:

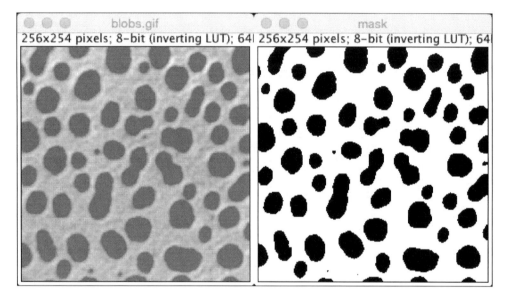

The red areas indicate the foreground, which are our potential particles, while everything else will be ignored. The goal will now be to segment the particles based on two main characteristics: their shape and size. We will finish this step by creating the mask by selecting **Edit | Selection | Create Mask** from the menu (the mask is the image on the right-hand side).

Before we start detecting the particles, we first need to know a few things about them. We need to know the size of the particles. There are two simple ways of determining the size of all the particles within this image, and we will start with the most straightforward one. To determine the size of a specific particle, we will just draw a region around it and measure it. In the section on area measurements, we used polygon selection to measure the area and shape descriptors. For particle analysis, we need to determine what the smallest particle is that we may still consider a real particle.

To get started, let's take the particle at (103,111) as the smallest real particle. After drawing a polygon around it, you may get an area of 363 pixels and a circularity of 0.9188. If we take a less circular particle, for instance at (133,83), we get an area of 434 and a circularity of 0.7329. Let's take the minimum value for each parameter of these two observations, giving us a minimum area of 363 pixels and a minimum circularity of 0.7329 to continue with. We can now perform particle analysis by selecting **Analyze | Analyze Particles...** from the menu. Enter the following parameters in the dialog that opens:

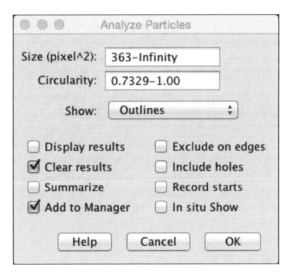

The size is the range of sizes that will be counted as particles, measured in square pixels (area). The circularity range that we found is now defined as the particles that are round or more round than our estimate. For the **Show** option, you can select multiple output types, including outlines. When you use the **Add to Manager** option, this output is not really required anymore and can be set to **Nothing**. When you do not wish to measure particles that are only partially in the image, you must select the **Exclude on edges** option. In *Chapter 9, Creating ImageJ Plugins for Analysis*, we will look at an implementation of particle analysis in a time series.

After clicking on **OK**, the particles will be added to the ROI Manager, at which point, segmenting the particles is completed. We can now measure the particles using the same methods for any other area selection that we looked at in the earlier sections. Another way of setting the parameters for area and circularity is to run the particle analysis, but without restrictions on either the size or circularity parameter. This will detect every particle within the image, and the results can be filtered after the segmentation. Both methods should give you similar results, with an equal amount of work.

Summary

In this chapter, we saw some methods to measure parameters within images and time series. We used some of the techniques used in the previous chapters to extract data from our images. You learned how to visualize dynamic data in a single image (kymographs). We looked at colocalization in a qualitative way, as a prelude to quantitative analysis later on in the book. Finally, we looked at particle analysis as a way to detect similar objects within a single image.

In the next chapter, you will use some of the techniques that you learned and apply them in macros to increase your efficiency.

6
Developing Macros in ImageJ

In this chapter, we will take a look at ways to automate our image processing to allow for faster and more efficient processing. The processing we did earlier was adequate, but time consuming. When dealing with very large stacks or time series, or with many individual files, the processing we performed was good but inefficient. We will look at macros in ImageJ and understand how they will help us with the processing. In this chapter, we will cover the following topics:

- Recording and running macros
- Modifying macros
- User input in macros
- Progress in macros
- Running macros in batch mode
- Installing macros

Recording macros

Macros are sets of commands that allow you to perform a series of tasks on a single image or multiple images. In a macro, you can place all the commands you can find in the ImageJ menu structure. A very basic application of a macro is to convert images from one specific type into another type. In order to create a macro, we could create one from scratch by typing all the commands in a text file, which we can then execute. However, if we are using commands from the menu structure, an easier way would be to use the macro recorder.

The macro recorder will register every command and selection you make, and place them in a simple editor. This is a very simple and fast way to create a macro that will perform a basic set of tasks on an image. To begin recording, go to **Plugins | Macros | Record...** from the menu, which will open a new recorder window:

The recorder window has a list to allow different types of recordings. The default is macro, but it is also possible to record commands for a plugin using Java as the recording type. ImageJ also supports JavaScript code and Beanshell scripts to run, and these types can also be created here. When JavaScript or BeanShell is selected, the commands recorded will look slightly different from the default macro commands. There is also an option to set the name of the new macro you are creating. Macros in ImageJ do not require an underscore in their names and have the .ijm extension to indicate that they are ImageJ macros. When you have performed all the processing steps you wish to unleash on your image, you can press the **Create** button to finalize the macro for saving.

Recording a macro for conversion

Let's take a look at a simple recording of a macro that will take a multichannel image, change the lookup table of the blue channel, and convert it to an RGB image. We will use the sample image of the HeLa cells. For better processing, we will not include the open image command. So, we will first open the image by going to **File | Open Samples | HeLa Cells**. We will then start the macro recorder by going to **Plugins | Macros | Record...** from the ImageJ menu. Make sure that the type is set to **Macro**, and enter a name for your macro. Next, we will perform the steps we wish to record in the order we wish to use them. To start with, activate the image window and select the blue channel by pressing the right arrow key twice. You will see that there are now two commands in the recorder window:

```
run("Next Slice [>]");
run("Next Slice [>]");
```

Note that when you click on the channel bar with the mouse, nothing will be recorded and no commands are added to the recorder window.

> The recorder does not record mouse clicks that change the state of the display. It does not record mouse clicks to change the channel, frames, or slices in stacks nor when you adjust the brightness/contrast. Only the **Set** and **Apply** commands will show up in the recorder.

With the blue channel selected, we will now change the LUT of this channel to **Cyan** by going to **Image | Lookup Tables | Cyan** from the menu. This will add a new command to the recorder, corresponding to the action we just performed:

```
run("Cyan");
```

We will now perform the last step in this process, which is converting the image to an RGB image. To do so, go to **Image | Type | RGB Color** from the menu. A new image will be created of the RGB type, and a new command is added to the recorder window:

```
run("RGB Color");
```

Now, we have a complete macro to convert a three-channel image into an RGB image, with a change of the LUT in one channel. The final recorder window will look like the following screenshot:

The name of the macro I have selected is `convert_3ch_rgb.ijm`. When you create the macro, this will be the default name used when you save the macro. When you push the **Create** button, a new window will open that will look a little different, depending on the distribution of ImageJ that you are using. When using Fiji, the **Script Editor** window will open, with the commands that we recorded in the editor:

The advantage of the Fiji script editor is that it has **syntax highlighting** (indicated by the colors for different elements) and line numbering. It also supports a tabbed interface, allowing multiple macros to be opened at the same time within the same window. This editor also has a run button at the bottom of the window to let you run the macro directly.

In the standard ImageJ distribution, the editor will look a little more basic, and it does not have the added features that the Fiji script editor provides:

Notice the lack of highlighting and the absence of line numbers in the editor. Once we have created the macro, we can run it using the keyboard shortcut *Ctrl + R* or by going to **Macros | Run** (standard ImageJ) or **Run | Run (Fiji)**.

The recording of the macro allows for many steps to be recorded in sequence. However, there is a drawback to the macro as we have it now: we need to open the image we want to process ourselves, and we need to save the resulting image as well. Furthermore, the macro in its current form only processes the currently active image. As long as only one image is open, this will not pose a problem. However, when we have more than one image open when we run the macro, we have to make sure that the window that we want to process is selected before we run the macro. In the next section, we will try to add some commands to deal with opening and closing images to allow for more robust processing.

Modifying macros

The macro we created in the previous section was effective. However, it does not deal with opening and closing images. So now, we will look at the process of modifying the current macro we now have. Most of the work will be done in the editor window, but we will still use the recorder window to discover the functions required to open and close images.

Let's start by adding an option to open the image you wish to process to the macro that we have. I will use the image we used earlier. However, since you are more likely to have images saved locally on a disk, we will save the **HeLa Cells** image to the local disk. Let's make a folder named `processing` on the desktop and store the **HeLa Cells** image in it. To save the image, go to **File | Save** or press *Ctrl + S* and select the folder on the desktop as the destination. After saving the image, we can start with the process of opening an image within our macro.

To start with, we need to make sure our previous macro is opened in the editor window and start the macro recorder. We also need to make sure that there are no images open. Now, we will start by opening the image we saved by selecting **File | Open…**. Then, we will select the image from the folder we created in the previous step. In the recorder window, we will now see a line that tells ImageJ to open the image. When done on our computer, `<username>` will be set to the user name that was used when you logged in:

```
open("/Users/<username>/Desktop/processing/hela-cells.tif");
```

This tells us that ImageJ requires the `open()` function with a single parameter, which is a line of text (called a `string`, delimited by double quotes in Java/ImageJ). This line of text contains the full path of the file you wish to open. To implement this command into our macro, we need to copy or type this command into the editor window on the first line. We can now test whether everything works as we expect by running the macro. To do so, we need to close the image and run the macro by selecting the editor window and pressing *Ctrl + R* to run the macro. If all goes well, the image will open, the blue channel will be selected and changed to cyan, and finally, the image will be converted to an RGB image.

Next, we will look at how to save the new image to the same folder but with a different name. We need to make sure the recorder window is still open, and then click on the newly created image to activate it. Next, we will save the image as a TIFF file by going to **File | Save**. We will keep the name as it was set by ImageJ. In the recorder window, we should now see a new line with the save command:

```
run("Save", "save=[/Users/<username>/Desktop/processing/hela-cells.tif
(RGB).tif]");
```

This command is a little more complex than the open command, as it uses the more general `run()` method. The run method takes two parameters: a string with the command, (in this case **Save**) and a string with the form `save=[]`, with the filename between the square brackets for saving. Note that the user name was replaced with `<username>` in this command. It should be changed to the user name of your logged-in account. We can now add this command to our script to perform the save function.

Next, to complete the process, we will close all the images that are currently open. To do so, we will select the recently saved image and close it. Alternatively, we will select **File | Close All** from the menu. If we close an image or use close all, the following line will be placed in the recorder window, respectively:

```
close();
run("Close All");
```

The first line means the currently active window will be closed, while the second command will close all open images. Since we want to close all the images that are open, when we are finished processing, the second command is more suited for our macro. We will add the `Close All` command to the script, which means our final macro will look as follows:

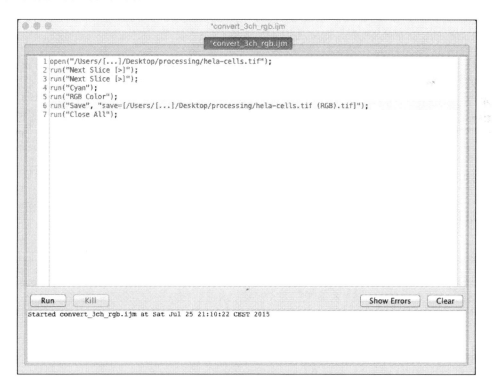

When using the script editor in Fiji, we can also see the runs that were performed with the current macro in the list below the editor. Using the **Clear** button allows us to reset this history. When you open this macro as it is now, it will open the image, change the LUT of the third channel, convert it to RGB, save the resulting image, and then close all the images. Even though this macro is very simple, it processes this image much faster than we will ever be able to do by hand. There is only one problem with this macro: it only works for a single image in a specific location. If we want to process many different images, this macro will not be very practical. We would have to manually change the macro for each file that we wish to process. So, in the next section, we will add the possibility for the user to select a file when the macro is run.

User input in macros

Our previous macro was very efficient at processing a specific image, but it would be more efficient if the macro asked for the file to be processed. To do this, we will need to add a method that will ask the user for a file. The only problem is that we cannot use the recorder to get this function. We need to find a function that asks the user for a file location, which can be done with the built-in macro functions available in ImageJ. On the ImageJ website, there is an extensive list of all the macro functions that you can access at `http://imagej.nih.gov/ij/developer/macro/functions.html`. The functions are sorted alphabetically.

Opening a specific file

The function we want is a file open dialog that asks the user to locate an image file. The easiest way to find a function on this page is to use the find function of your browser to search for relevant keywords. To find the function we need, we will use the search term "file open dialog" in the search box. When we enter the search term, there will be multiple occurrences on the page, so we will look at all the descriptions for each occurrence. In this case, the function that describes what we need is a function called `File.openDialog(title)`, and the description says that it will display a file open dialog that returns the path of the file that the user selects. We will now change our current macro to use this function to allow us to change any file that we select. We will change the first line of our macro into the following two lines:

```
fname = File.openDialog("Select 3 channel image");
open(fname);
```

The first line tells ImageJ to display a file open dialog with the title **Select 3 channel image** and then store the path that the user selected in a variable called `fname`. On the next line, we modified the `open()` command to use the `fname` variable to open the image that the user selected. One thing to note in this example is that the variable type is not specified. Macros in ImageJ are weakly typed and do not require that you specify the type beforehand.

Saving an image to a folder

So now, we made the macro a little bit more flexible. We can now select any file we wish at any location on the hard disk or attached storage. The only problem is that the image is still saved to a fixed location with a fixed name. So now, we have to change the portion of our macro that deals with saving the image. There are many possible solutions to this problem. We can save the new image in the same folder as the image we opened, or we could save it in a different folder where we collect all the processed images. We will start with the first option: saving it to the same folder as the image that we opened.

To get the name of the folder we selected, we can use a function called `File.directory()`, which will give us the directory of the last file that was opened using a file open dialog. This is exactly what we need for our save function, so let's start by adding this function in our code. To do so, we will add a new line before the `run("Save", …)` command and add the following code:

```
fdir = File.directory();
```

This will store the path of the last opened image in a variable named `fdir`. In order to save a file, we need the path but also the filename of the new file. The filename in this case is just the title of the created image, so we will use a function to get the title of the current image by adding this line underneath the `fdir` line:

```
newName = getTitle();
```

We will store the value of the new filename in a variable named `newName`. We are now ready to modify the `save` function to use the two variables that we created. What we need to do is combine the `fdir` and `newName` variables. We can do this within the `save` command, so we will change the old `save` command to the following line:

```
run("Save", "save=["+fidr+newName+".tif]");
```

We have replaced the path that was specified between the square brackets with the two variables. We had to add a set of quotes between the square brackets to interrupt the string, and we used the + operator to concatenate the strings. We specified the extension of the file we wished to save. As the title of the image does not contain an extension at the end of the name, we need to add it. Alternatively, we could use the saveAs macro command to achieve the same result (adding the extension is not required because we will save the image as a TIFF file):

```
saveAs("Tiff", fdir+newName);
```

> In this case, the RGB Color command creates a new image. When calling Save on a new image, we can change the name, and it will work the same way as the saveAs command. If your function does not create a new image but you would still like to store the result as a separate file, use the saveAs command. Otherwise, the save function will overwrite the image on the disk with the modified data.

Our macro should now look like this:

Our macro is now more flexible. We can select any file for processing, and the result will be stored in the same folder as the original but with a modified name. The next step is to modify the code to control which channel will be modified.

Adding choices

Our macro now allows us to modify any image that we can locate and save the result in the same folder. In the next step, we will ask the user which channel we wish to change. We need to ask the user for a number between 1 and 3, which will be the channel that will be updated. There are two basic ways of retrieving a number: we could use a text field where the user can enter a number, or we could present a list of numbers where the user can select the correct one. The first method is very easy, but also requires additional checking. What if the user enters a value larger than the number of channels (or not a number at all)? A slightly safer method is to give the user a limited set of choices where only one can be selected.

We will use a set of functions related to creating a dialog and adding fields to it. We will need to place this code somewhere at the beginning of the macro, before we call the next slice command. We will place the following code directly after the open command:

```
Dialog.create("Select a channel");
Dialog.addChoice("Channel number:", newArray("1","2","3"));
Dialog.show();
```

The first line will create a dialog with the title Select a channel. Next, we added a choice list to the newly created dialog with an array containing the options 1, 2, and 3 as strings. Finally, we called the show() method to display the dialog we created.

We created a dialog that asks the user to select a channel number, but we did not use the selection yet. If we run the code as it is now, the result would be the same regardless of the selection we make in the dialog. So, our next step is to retrieve the user selection and extract the number that the user selected. The function to do this is getChoice(), which is part of the dialog function. We will add it directly after the show command as follows:

```
chChoice = Dialog.getChoice();
```

This command will store the selected choice in a variable called chChoice. However, if we look at the description of the function, this function returns a string. This is a problem, because we need it to be a number in order to select the correct slice. There is a function available to convert a string to an integer in the macro language. It is called parseInt(), and we can implement it as follows:

```
sliceNumber = parseInt(chChoice);
```

The `sliceNumber` variable now contains the user's channel selection. Next, we will use this number to select the correct slice in our image. We could use a small loop combined with our next slice commands. However, there is a faster and simpler method using a built-in macro function called `setSlice()`. To do this, replace the two lines with `run("Next Slice [>]")` with the following line:

```
setSlice(sliceNumber);
```

If we wish to also change the color of the lookup table that will be used, we could add a second choice list to our dialog using the same methodology. We could just add another `addChoice()` command, but this time, with several choices of LUTs (for example, cyan, yellow, magenta, and so on). The `getChoice()` function retrieves the results of each choice list in the order they are added to the dialog. If you add the LUT choice after the channel number, it would be retrieved with the second call to `getChoice()`. Our macro will now look as follows (I have added the color choice as well):

```
fname = File.openDialog("Select 3 channel image");
open(fname);
Dialog.create("Select a channel");
Dialog.addChoice("Channel number:",newArray("1","2","3")));
Dialog.addChoice("Select color:", newArray("Cyan","Magenta","Yell
ow"));
Dialog.show();
chChoice  =Dialog.getChoice();
clrChoice = Dialog.getChoice();
sliceNumber = parseInt(chChoice);
setSlice(sliceNumber);
run(clrChoice);
run("RGB Color");
fdir = File.directory();
newName = getTitle();
run("Save", "save=["+fdir+newName+".tif]");
run("Close All");
```

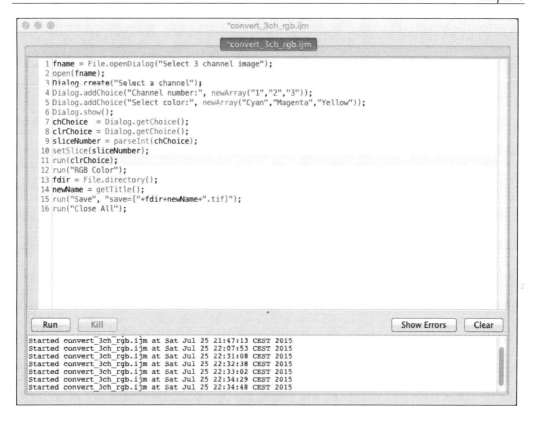

```
 1 fname = File.openDialog("Select 3 channel image");
 2 open(fname);
 3 Dialog.create("Select a channel");
 4 Dialog.addChoice("Channel number:", newArray("1","2","3"));
 5 Dialog.addChoice("Select color:", newArray("Cyan","Magenta","Yellow"));
 6 Dialog.show();
 7 chChoice  = Dialog.getChoice();
 8 clrChoice = Dialog.getChoice();
 9 sliceNumber = parseInt(chChoice);
10 setSlice(sliceNumber);
11 run(clrChoice);
12 run("RGB Color");
13 fdir = File.directory();
14 newName = getTitle();
15 run("Save", "save=["+fdir+newName+".tif]");
16 run("Close All");
```

[Run] [Kill]   [Show Errors] [Clear]

```
Started convert_3ch_rgb.ijm at Sat Jul 25 21:47:13 CEST 2015
Started convert_3ch_rgb.ijm at Sat Jul 25 22:07:53 CEST 2015
Started convert_3ch_rgb.ijm at Sat Jul 25 22:31:08 CEST 2015
Started convert_3ch_rgb.ijm at Sat Jul 25 22:32:38 CEST 2015
Started convert_3ch_rgb.ijm at Sat Jul 25 22:33:02 CEST 2015
Started convert_3ch_rgb.ijm at Sat Jul 25 22:34:29 CEST 2015
Started convert_3ch_rgb.ijm at Sat Jul 25 22:34:48 CEST 2015
```

There is now a new variable called clrChoice, which holds the value of the color selection that the user makes. If you run the modified macro, you would have to select the image you wish to process and then set the channel and LUT color. After this, the image will be processed according to the values you set. The macro is now quite flexible and allows for different types of conversions of a specific channel with a specific color. We now only need one more modification to make it a little more robust. We need to check whether the image that the user selected actually has three channels or not.

Performing input checking

To add a check for the number of slices in the selected image, we need a simple conditional statement. The `if` statement will perform this check. We will add this conditional after we open the image, but before we ask the user for input. If there are less than three channels, we need to stop the execution of the macro and close the image we opened:

```
if(nSlices<3) {
run("Close All");
exit("Not enough channels in the image (min. is 3)!");
}
```

The `nSlices` function is a built-in macro function that returns the number of slices of the current image. We will check the value of the number of slices against the value that we require. If there are insufficient channels, we would close all images and abort the macro using the `exit()` function.

When using the `nSlices` function, remember that ImageJ calculates this value by multiplying the number of slices, frames, and channels of an image. When working with (hyper)stacks, the `nSlices` function does not return the value you might expect. For example, a 5D image with two channels, five slices, and 51 frames will return a value of 510 (*2*5*51*). For stacks, you can use the `Stack` methods. To count the number of channels, you can use the `Stack.getDimensions()` function.

There are two forms of the exit function: one without a parameter and one with a string parameter. The string parameter will display a message indicating why the macro was aborted. It is recommended that you use the latter form to make a user understand why the macro is not performing a task by providing feedback. Our macro should now look like this:

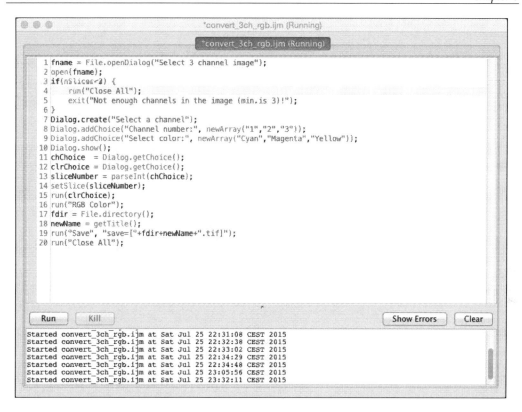

Our macro is now robust and will run in a predictable way every time we run it. If our image has very few slices, it would abort. If it has more slices, it would run correctly. However, we will be unable to modify any slice beyond the third slice. So, our final modification will check for the number of slices in the image and adjust our choices accordingly by manipulating the array of slice numbers.

To change the content of the choice list, we first need to create an array that is slightly longer than the one that is currently specified. We want to limit the number of channels somewhat, so we will create an array with five channels as a maximum. We will also adjust the check for the number of channels to reflect this alteration. We will start by creating an array containing numbers 1 through 5 as strings and modify the conditional statement:

```
chNumbers = newArray("1","2","3","4","5");
if(nSlices>chNumbers.length) {
   run("Close All");
   exit("The many channels in the image (max is"+chNumbers.
length+")!");
}
```

This will store the channel numbers in the chNumbers array, and the conditional array will now check whether the number of slices is not larger than the length of that array. This method allows us to easily enter additional channel numbers in the future to the array, without having to modify any other code.

Next, we added the list of channel numbers to our choice list in the dialog. However, we have to take into account that the user can select an image with fewer channels than five, so we need to change the array that we add to the choice list to reflect the number of channels that are present in the selected image. To do this, we can use the trim function that works on arrays. The trim function takes two parameters: the first one is the array, and the second one is an integer that specifies the number of elements that need to be returned, starting from the first element. We can use the nSlices function to give us the number of elements we want the trim function to return:

```
Dialog.addChoice("Channel number:", Array.trim(chNumbers, nSlices));
```

If we now run the modified macro on our **HeLa Cells** file, we would see that the choice list for the channel number only contains the values 1, 2, and 3, which is exactly what we would expect for this image. If we opened another image with five channels, we could choose from five options in the list. You can try this by saving the **Neuron (1.6M 5 channels)** sample image to test this. The final macro will now look like the following screenshot:

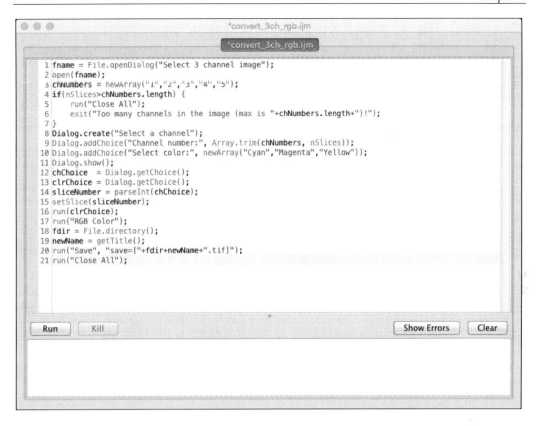

```
 1 fname = File.openDialog("Select 3 channel image");
 2 open(fname);
 3 chNumbers = newArray("1","2","3","4","5");
 4 if(nSlices>chNumbers.length) {
 5     run("Close All");
 6     exit("Too many channels in the image (max is "+chNumbers.length+")!");
 7 }
 8 Dialog.create("Select a channel");
 9 Dialog.addChoice("Channel number:", Array.trim(chNumbers, nSlices));
10 Dialog.addChoice("Select color:", newArray("Cyan","Magenta","Yellow"));
11 Dialog.show();
12 chChoice  = Dialog.getChoice();
13 clrChoice = Dialog.getChoice();
14 sliceNumber = parseInt(chChoice);
15 setSlice(sliceNumber);
16 run(clrChoice);
17 run("RGB Color");
18 fdir = File.directory();
19 newName = getTitle();
20 run("Save", "save=["+fdir+newName+".tif]");
21 run("Close All");
```

Run   Kill   Show Errors   Clear

For the next step in processing using macros, we will create a macro that will perform processing steps on a list of files contained within a folder. This process will require some form of progress to let the user know that something is happening and to give a hint of how long the processing will take.

Showing progress in macros

In the previous sections, we saw that we can process a single image file using a (relatively) simple macro. Although the macro is quite flexible, it still requires the user to select each file individually and to set the values each time. Many times, you wish to perform the same processing steps on a collection of many similar images. The images have the same specifications (number of channels, colors, and so on) but are of different samples or individuals. When processing large numbers of images, it is useful to show progress to indicate how far we are in the processing and provide some visual feedback of how many items have been processed. The easiest type of feedback is to present the percentage of files that have been processed. Any value lower than 100 percent indicates that we are not done yet. If we keep track of how long it takes to process 10 percent of the images, we can (roughly) estimate the time required to finish the processing. Another useful type of feedback is to provide a message at the end of processing that we are finished.

For this section, we will create a different macro that will take a folder with time series images, each containing 20 frames and two channels. We will take the first channel of each image and create an average projection of the first five frames and save the result in the same folder. We will then take the second channel of each image, create a maximum projection, and store it in the same folder as well. The folder will contain 10 files that need to be processed, as well as a single text file that contains a description of the files in the folder. We will start by creating a macro for the processing steps in the next section.

Processing the time series

We will begin by creating the steps to perform the processing. We can use the recorder as well as the built-in macro function reference page in the ImageJ website to help us with the processing. We will first open the image in ImageJ in the regular way. The code to open the images one by one from a folder will be written later on. Once the image is open, we will create the code that will process each channel. I will introduce some useful constructs that will make the code a little more clear. I will add comments to the code to indicate what is happening, and I will encapsulate the processing in functions.

Let's start by creating a function that will generate the average projection of the green channel and save it. Creating a function in an ImageJ macro is very simple. To declare a function, we will use the `function` keyword, followed by the name of the function and the parameter list. For our green channel, the function declaration is as follows:

```
function processGreenChannel() {

}
```

The function is called `processGreenChannel` and has no parameters (this will change later on, but for now it is fine). Our first processing step is to generate an average of the green channel. There are many ways of doing this, but for now, we will use the most basic one. We will create an average for both channels and remove the channel we do not want before saving. To create an average projection, we need the recorder to discover the format of the command. Start the recorder by going to **Plugins | Macros | Record...** if it is not already open. Next, we will go to **Image | Stacks | Z Project...** from the menu and enter 5 for **Stop slice**, and **Average intensity** for the method. We will see that the command that gives us the result is shown in the recorder:

```
run("Z Project...", "stop=5 projection=[Average Intensity]");
```

This will be the first command we will add to our function to process the green channel. Next, we wish to remove the red channel from this average projection. To do this, we will go to **Image | Stacks | Delete Slice** from the menu. A dialog will open, giving us a choice to delete the channel (there is not really a choice here). By pressing **OK**, the first channel (the red one) will be removed. The recorder shows us that the command used for this is the following one:

```
run("Delete Slice", "delete=channel");
```

We can add the same code we used to save the image in our previous macro to apply here as well. Our function will now look as follows:

```
function processGreenChannel() {
  //create an average projection of the first 5 frames
  run("Z Project...","stop=5 projection=[Average Intensity]");
  //delete the red channel
  run("Delete Slice","delete=channel");
  //save the new image
  fdir = File.directory();
  fname = getTitle();
  run("Save","save=["+fdir+fname+"]");
  //close the saved image
  close();
}
```

Notice that we do not require the extension at the end of the name. The projection command used a prefix to change the name (AVG_), and our original image already had an extension at the end, which was preserved by the projection command. The final step in the processing of the green channel is to close the image we have created and saved. This time, however, we cannot use the close all command, as we are not done yet with the processing of the original image. We will just use the close command, which only closes the currently active image as indicated by the last line of our function. I have included single-line comments in the function to indicate what is going to happen in the next line(s) as an aid to understanding what will happen next. This is a very basic programming tool that can save a lot of time when we examine our code after weeks or months. Single-line comments are indicated by text preceded by two forward slashes. If you need more text over multiple lines for readability, there are multiline comments, which start with /* and end with */:

```
//single-line comment
/*
multi line comment
that is spread over
several lines.
*/
```

The function we will create for our red channel is very similar, except we will now use a different projection method. Also, we must delete a different channel compared to the previous function. The complete function to process the red channel is as follows:

```
functionprocessRedChannel() {
    //create the maximum projection
    run("Z Project...","projection=[Max Intensity]");
    //select the green channel (which is number 2)
    setSlice(2);
    //delete the green channel
    run("Delete","delete=channel");
    //save the new image
    fdir  =File.directory();
    fname = getTitle();
    run("Save","save=["+fdir+fname+"]");
    //close the new image
    close();
}
```

There are only two minor alterations compared to the processing of the green channel. The type of projection was changed from `Average Intensity` to `Max Intensity`, and the `setSlice` command was added to select the green channel before calling the delete channel function. Note that if we also wanted to perform a measurement on each of the channels, we could add some measurement code or a function call before the `close()` statement to perform the measurement on the selected channel.

Now that we have completed the processing code for each channel, we can already see that there are many similarities between the two functions. It would be possible to create a single function that will process each channel accordingly using a few input parameters. In this case, you would need three parameters: one for the stop point you wish to use for the projection, one for the type of projection, and one for the slice number you wish to remove. We could do this for the current function, but it may be simpler to keep separate functions. If we want to change something in the green channel, processing it might mean we have to introduce even more parameters to the function to make it work. This would make the function call very complex. Therefore, it is easier to keep two separate functions. The only parameter that would be useful in this context is the directory where the image will be saved. As we will write code to process an entire directory, we will have the path to that folder already present, so we can easily add it as a parameter. We will modify the function definition as follows for the green channel processing function:

```
function processGreenChannel(fdir) {
...
}
```

This means that we can remove (or comment out) the line that provides a value to `fdir` within the body of the function:

```
//fdir  =File.directory();
```

In this case, I've commented out the line instead of removing it. This is generally a good practice if it involves only a few lines, as it shows how the function should work and what the function of the variable is. However, this is not advised for large sections, as the code will become very long with dead code that you need to skip.

Our next step will deal with selecting the folder to create a list of files that need to be processed. For the sake of overview, we will also create a function for this part. The first step in this function will be to ask the user for a folder that contains the files that need to be processed. When we search the reference web page, we will find a function called getDirectory(string) that provides the functionality we need. In the description, there is also a reference to the getFileList function. This function will return a list of files in a specified directory path. We need both of them for our folder processing function, which will look as follows:

```
function processFolder() {
  //get a folder for processing
  fdir = getDirectory();
  //create a list of files that we need to process
  flist = getFileList(fdir);
}
```

The point where we add this function description is not important for the processing in our macro. The declaration can be anywhere within the macro, but I will place it at the beginning of the code. It makes sense to place the function declarations in the order that you expect them to be called.

At this point, it might be useful to introduce a simple tool that is available to debug macros in ImageJ: the **log window**. The log window is a text window that can print the value of a variable, allowing you to see whether the value is what you expect it to be. It can also be used as a reference for the user to see which folders have been processed, thus avoiding a folder being processed more than once. We will add a log call to our function, showing the folder that is being processed as well as the number of files that are present in that folder. Placing the following lines directly below the flist statement will result in the following output:

```
//display the folder and the number of files
IJ.log("Current folder: "+fdir);
IJ.log("Nr of files: "+flist.length);
```

The last step is to go over each of the files and run our processing functions on the image that we open. To do this, we will use a basic loop structure, the for loop:

```
//go over all the files in the file list
for(i=0; i<flist.length; i++) {
  //get the full file name
  fname = fdir + flist[i];
  //open the image specified by fname
  open(fname);
  //process each channel
  processGreenChannel(fdir);
```

```
    processRedChannel(fdir);
    //close all images when we are done
    run("Close All");
}
```

We ended the loop with a `Close All` statement to make sure that all images are closed before we go on to the next file.

 Fiji also provides a small list of templates that allow a general framework for image processing in macros. For Fiji, two templates are very useful. The first is the **Process Folder** template (**Templates | IJ1 Macro | Process Folder**), which can be used for the same purpose as I am using for this example. The other template is the **Scale All ROIs** template (**Templates | IJ1 Macro | Scale All ROIs**). This template tells us how to go over a list of ROIs in the ROI manager and alter the size of the ROIs.

For this loop, we might also want to show the processing progress to indicate how many files we have processed. To do this, we will add a call to the `showProgress()` function, which takes a single parameter between `0` and `1`, indicating the fraction of files that have been processed. We can place the call directly after the `close all` command:

```
//show the progress
showProgress((i+1)/flist.length);
```

As arrays in Java are zero-based, we added a value of `1` to the index to indicate the file number that was processed. The progress bar will be shown in the bottom-right corner of the ImageJ window. This completes the macro to process an entire folder, except that in the current state, we will still have two problems when we wish to run it. We only have function definitions, but we don't have any direct calls to those functions. We are missing the entry point for our macro. This point is easily resolved by adding a call to our `processFolder` function at the beginning of the macro.

The second problem is a little harder to solve. As specified at the beginning of this section, we also have a text file in the folder we wish to process. If we run the code as it is now, this text file would also be opened by our macro. This will result in an error when we try to process our channels using our functions. If our text file was the last file being processed, this would not be a huge problem (just a little sloppy). However, when our text file is in the beginning or somewhere halfway, the macro will terminate at an undetermined point, and we would have to manually correct it. This would negate the entire benefit of having a macro to process a folder. It will result in us still having to manually go over each file.

We could solve the problem by removing the text file from our folder, which may be a good solution if it is only one folder. However, if you have many folders that you wish to process, this method would not be very useful. Also, deleting the text file means you will lose the information that was contained within it, which might be important. Another option would be to create a subfolder in your processing folder and place the text file there. There is a problem with this solution as well. Folders are also seen by Java as types of files. When creating the file list, the subfolder would still be included. Trying to open the subfolder using the open command might have unexpected side effects.

We can solve all these problems by adding a conditional statement inside the loop that checks the type of file that we are currently processing. This `if` statement needs to check two conditions: whether the current file a directory and whether it is an image. To do this, we will add the following `if` statement around our open and process commands:

```
//verify that this file is correct
if(!File.isDirectory(fname) && endsWith(flist[i], ".tif")) {
   ...
}
```

This `if` statement checks whether the full path stored in the `fname` variable is not a directory and the current file name ends with `.tif`. This check will exclude any directories from being processed as well as any file that does not have the `.tif` extension. The `showProgress` call can stay outside of the `if` statement. The completed macro can be downloaded from the Packt Publishing's website for comparison (`batch_project.ijm`). When we run the macro, we will see that processing occurs fairly rapidly and the progress bar in the main ImageJ window is displayed while the processing occurs. Depending on the number of images and the processing power of your computer, processing might go too fast to see everything.

There is one argument that we can add to the current macro. This argument may speed up the process and also prevent all the images being shown when they're being processed. This can be controlled using the following command:

```
setBatchMode(true);
```

When the batch mode is set to `true`, the images will not be shown, and only the newly created images will be visible. If the value is set to `false`, the images will be shown. By setting the batch mode to `true`, a 20-fold speed increase can be achieved in some cases. In the next section, we will look at another way to run a macro over multiple files using the built-in method that comes with ImageJ: batch process mode.

Running macros in batch process mode

In the previous sections, we looked at processing a folder using a macro with different processing functions. The method described earlier is very flexible and powerful, and allows a great deal of control over the processing flow and what will be processed. ImageJ, however, also has a method that can perform a similar task, which is the batch process command. This command allows you to run a specified macro that you created over a folder and allows you to store the results in the same or a different folder. To start the batch process command, go to **Process | Batch | Macro...** in the ImageJ menu, which will open the following dialog:

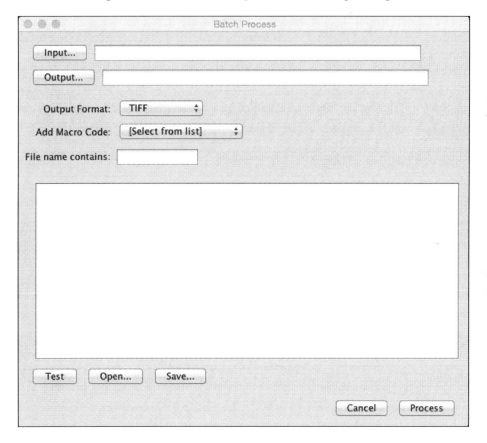

You can set the input and output folders using the buttons. You can also set the output format. If you don't set the output folder, the image would not be saved unless you saved it within your own code. You can use one of the macros that come with ImageJ using the **Add Macro Code** selector, or you can use the **Open...** button to load your own code file. To specify that you only wish to process image files, you could use the **File name contains** field to specify a pattern that indicates you only wish to process TIFF files by typing (.tif) with the brackets included. When you press the **Process** button, the code that is shown in the text field will be run for each image that matches the pattern.

Note that your macro needs to conform to a few rules to be able to use it in the batch mode. If you wish to perform the saving yourself inside the macro, you need to place code to save the results in your macro and leave the **Output** field in the **Batch Process** dialog empty. To perform the same task that we did in our previous macro, we will copy the entire code to the **Batch Process** dialog. Then, we will remove the processFolder() function and the function call, replace it with a line that gives us the current directory of the opened image, and then call the processing functions:

```
fdir = File.directory();
processGreenChannel(fdir);
processRedChannel(fdir);

//processing functions...
```

We can leave the output field in the process dialog empty, as images are saved inside our processing functions. We can add (.tif) to the **File name contains** field to ensure that the text file will be skipped. When we click the **Process** button, the folder will be processed in a similar way, and the results will be stored as we described in our macro's processing functions.

Both methods are very suitable for processing entire folders, and the results are similar. The biggest difference is that the **Batch Process** mode allows slightly less control over the processing steps, and it does not allow recursive processing of folders and subfolders. Also, it is not possible to include multiple user inputs or dialogs before the folder is processed. The code within the **Batch Process** command needs to be self-sufficient. Any user input will have to be entered every iteration.

Installing macros

Once you have created your macro, you can save it in the macros folder within the ImageJ folder. When you wish to run your macro, you can go to **Plugins | Macros | Open** or **Plugins | Macros | Run** to open and run your macro. It is also possible to add your macros to the macros menu. You can do this by installing a macro in ImageJ by selecting **Plugins | Macros | Install...** from the menu. Once you have selected your macro, it will be added at the bottom of the macros menu. It is also possible to add your macro to the StartupMacros.txt file in the macros folder. All macros mentioned in this file will be added to the macros menu automatically.

 Note that in Fiji, when you use the install option, the macro is only added for the duration of the session. As soon as you restart Fiji, the macro menu will be reset to the default content. It is, therefore, advised that you always place your macros and script in the macros or scripts folder of Fiji. To always load it when Fiji runs, use the StartupMacros.fiji.ijm file as described in the following code.

If you wish to make a toolbar button with a list of your macros that you often use, you can do so by modifying the StartupMacros.txt file (or StartupMacros.fiji.ijm file for Fiji). This could be very handy if you have multiple macros that you use frequently. To add your macros as a toolbar menu, add the following structure somewhere in the startup file:

```
var myTools = newMenu("My awesome tools",
newArray("Macro_1", "Macro_2", "-", "Macro_3"));

macro"My awesome tools - C037T0b11MT7b09aTcb09t" {
  cmd = getArgument();
  if(cmd== "Macro_1")
  runMacro("/PATH/TO/Macro_1_tool");
  else if(cmd == "Macro_2)"
  runMacro("/PATH/TO/some_other_tool");
}
```

The first argument for the `newMenu` method is a name for your menu item; in this case, I used `My awesome tools`. The second argument adds an array of macro commands to the menu, which will be displayed within the toolbar menu when added. If you add a dash in the array, a horizontal divider will be added to the menu at that location. This can be useful to group macros with similar functions. After defining the menu, we can implement the menu items using an `if...else` structure, where we compare the command that was selected using the `getArgument` method to see which tool needs to be launched. If we want to know the command necessary to run our macro, we can start the macro recorder and then go to **Plugins | Macros | Run...**, select our macro, and see what the command for our macro is.

It is also possible to add an icon to our menu, which needs to be specified as a string behind our macro implementation. This string consists of instructions to draw elements that we specify using a letter followed by coordinates. For instance, if we wish to write the string **Mat** (**My awesome tools**), we could use the following string for the icon:

```
C037T0b11MT7b09aTcb09t
```

The underlined characters are the letters we wish to add, while the value preceding it is the font size in points (`11`, `09`, and `09`, respectively). The alphabet `T` indicates that a character must be drawn, and the value next to it indicates the position of the character. It is also possible to draw a polygon using the following format (this requires ImageJ 1.48k):

```
Gxyxy...xy00
```

Drawing this icon can be somewhat complicated, and in Fiji, there is a **Beanshell** script that can convert an image to a toolbar icon string. This can be used by opening an image and going to **Plugins | Examples | Image To Tool Icon**. There is also an alternative that provides more flexibility and higher quality buttons in a separate toolbar. This alternative is **ActionBar** by *Jerome Mutterer*, which is a plugin that creates separate toolbars that can be set up to your own liking. It also supports icons in the PNG format.

Documentation for ActionBar can be found at `http://imagejdocu.tudor.lu/doku.php?id=plugin:utilities:action_bar:start`. It also contains an example of how to create your own toolbar and how to auto-load your tool bar when you start ImageJ.

Summary

In this chapter, you looked at how to create a macro using the recorder to discover commands and functions that we could apply. We made a basic macro that processed an image and generated a new image. Next, we looked at processing a folder full of images and created resulting images that were saved to a disk. Finally, we looked at batch process mode that allows ImageJ to process a folder in a similar way. In the next chapter, we will take a closer look at the constructs available for developing plugins and how to set up an environment for developing plugins.

7
Explanation of ImageJ Constructs

In the previous chapter, we developed macros to ease our processing and measurements. We used some techniques and constructs that are particular for the macro language in ImageJ. In this chapter, we will look at the following topics, in preparation to develop our own plugins:

- Frameworks for macros and plugins
- Special classes in ImageJ
- Built-in functions for macros
- API functions
- Setting up the NetBeans IDE for development
- Setting up for development using Maven

Frameworks for macros and plugins

We will look at some tools that ImageJ offers developers to deal with images and their processing. In the previous chapter, we looked at macros to perform common image-processing steps. This was already an improvement over the processing of time series one frame at a time, but ImageJ supports more tools and constructs that allow you to expand these basic tools further. In this chapter, we will look at some of these constructs as a preparation for the upcoming chapters, where we will look at plugins and their implementation.

ImageJ has two ways to process in a more automated fashion: macros and plugins. Besides the macros described in the previous chapter, ImageJ also supports other Java-based scripting languages such as Beanshell and JavaScript, as well as the scripting languages Python and Ruby, among others. The plugins can be split into two groups as well: plugins based on the original ImageJ (that is, ImageJ1.x plugins) and those based on the next development of ImageJ called **ImageJ2** (ImageJ2 plugins). The ImageJ2 development is designed to be backward compatible with ImageJ1.x, although this may change in the future. In this chapter, we will look at some of the constructs available when creating scripts and plugins. We will start by looking at the scripting languages supported by ImageJ.

Macros and scripting languages

As we saw in the previous chapter, we can easily create an ImageJ macro by starting the macro recorder and performing different steps for image processing and measurements. We set the type to Macro in the recorder. We can do the same thing for two other scripting languages that ImageJ supports: **BeanShell** and **JavaScript**. BeanShell scripts are a type of macros, but have access to the full ImageJ and Java API. This means, besides the commands available in macros, you can also use classes and interfaces from Java, providing much more options in processing. The advantage of the BeanShell scripting language is that it is an interpreted language (it does not have to be compiled before it can be run) and requires only an interpreter that has a small footprint. This makes it easy to create fast solutions and prototyping for plugins. In the following sections, I will examine some of the concepts in the BeanShell scripting language. Note that similar results can be achieved in the JavaScript language within ImageJ, where the only difference is small changes in syntax.

BeanShell scripting

BeanShell scripting allows you to create a script with all the advantages of a macro, but with the added benefit of having access to the Java API. You can use Java code almost directly as is. However, there are a few small differences. BeanShell scripts have weak typing. This means, you do not need to declare the variable type, and you can change the type of a variable on-the-fly. In all other ways, it is comparable to developing Java code. If you wish to use a class or interface from the Java API, you need to import it first using the following line of code:

```
import java.awt.event.KeyListener;
```

This import statement tells the script interpreter that it needs to load the KeyListener class from the java.awt.event package. This will allow you to monitor key presses. The KeyListener class is an interface that can be attached to an instance of a script. The class will generate an event when a key is pressed, resulting in a call to the keyPressed() method, which has to be overwritten by the script. Using the keyPressed() method, you can perform a specific task when a certain key is pressed.

The BeanShell scripting language also supports importing existing scripts into a new script. This way, you can daisy-chain multiple scripts. Daisy-chaining scripts means you use one script's output as input for the next script and so on. The advantage of this type of processing is that each script becomes a module that can be reused and combined in different ways to achieve different results. To import an existing script into your script, use the following syntax:

```
this.interpreter.source("some_script.bsh");
```

This will load the BeanShell script called some_script.bsh and give you access to its methods. A simple BeanShell script may consist of a series of basic ImageJ commands, but can also contain classes, functions, and even graphical user interfaces. We will now look at a few constructs used in the BeanShell scripting language that deal with ImageJ, images, and selections.

ImageJ main class

To access the main ImageJ window, we can use the IJ class to get the current instance of ImageJ. We can use this instance to gain access to some parameters that are provided by the ImageJ class:

```
protected ImageJ ij;
ij = IJ.getInstance();
Label status = ij.statusLine;
status.setText("Now we modified the status line text!");
```

In this short example, we created a variable of type ImageJ and stored a reference to the current instance of the ImageJ window in this variable, called ij. Next, we extracted the content of the ImageJ status line and stored it in a variable called status. Finally, we set the text of the status line to Now we modified the status line text!. Of course, this example is neither directly useful nor complete, but it shows you how to get access to the main ImageJ interface and modify a component of the interface.

I used two different ways of declaring and instantiating a variable: the `ij` variable was first declared and then instantiated, while the `status` variable was declared and instantiated in one line. The former would be required if your variable requires an extended scope (that is, across a loop or an entire class).

It is also possible to use the `IJ` class to execute commands that are part of the ImageJ menu structure using the `run()` method or methods such as `openImage()` to load images:

```
import ij.IJ;
IJ.run("In [+]", "");
imp = IJ.openImage("http://imagej.nih.gov/ij/images/blobs.gif");
```

The second line shows you how to zoom in once using the `run()` method from the `IJ` class. The third line shows you how to open an image using the `openImage()` method, which stores a reference to the image in a variable named `imp` in this example. To gain access to an image from within a BeanShell script, we can use the `openImage()`, as described earlier, to open an image. Alternatively, we could use the current active image (if there is an opened image):

```
imp = IJ.getImage();
```

Note that in Fiji, which uses the ImageJ2 release candidate, it is required that you add the import statement before using the `IJ` class' methods. In ImageJ1.x, these packages are auto-loaded and the import statement is optional. To make sure your scripts are future proof, it is best practice to include the import statements.

Functions to process images

Using the ImageJ class, you have access to the currently active image as well as to the methods to open images. There are also methods that allow you to process images on a pixel level using the `ImageProcessor` class. This class provides methods that can modify the image at the pixel level: either a single pixel or a group of pixels. The following snippet shows you how to use the `ImageProcessor` class to change the value of a specific pixel:

```
import ij.IJ;
import ij.process.ImageProcessor;

imp = IJ.openImage("http://imagej.nih.gov/ij/images/blobs.gif");
ip = imp.getProcessor();
ip.invertLut();
imp.setProcessor(ip);
ip.putPixel(64,128, 255);
```

In this example, we opened the **Blobs** sample image and got `ImageProcessor`. We then inverted the LUT (the **Blobs** image uses an inverted LUT when opened) and put the inverted image back in the `imp` object. Finally, we set the value for the pixel at the coordinates (x = 64, y = 128) to a value of 255. In this example, you will see a white pixel in one of the blobs at the location (64,128).

If the active image is an 8-bit image (as is the case for the **Blobs** image), this would result in a white pixel. In a 16-bit image this operation would result in a dark-gray pixel. If you want to know if the current image is a gray scale image and how many bits per pixel (8, 16, 24, or 32) it has, you could include the following commands:

```
bGray = ip.isGrayscale();
bitDepth = ip.getBitDepth();
```

This will allow you to determine exactly what kind of image you are dealing with. If `bGray` is `true`, the image is an 8,16, or 32 float grayscale image or a 24-bit image with identical values for the pixels in the red, green, and blue channels. The `bitDepth` value will tell you which level it is. The distinction is small, but significant. A 24-bit image that contains color information is not the same as a 24-bit image that is gray. The latter can be converted to an 8-bit image without loss of information, while the former cannot be converted to an 8-bit image without losing the color information.

Functions for selections

To gain access to selections in the ROI Manager, BeanShell scripts allow you to get an instance of the ROI Manager, which can then be used to extract the ROIs and use them for processing. The following code snippet takes the ROIs from the ROI Manager and enlarges them by 2 pixels:

```
import ij.IJ;
import ij.plugin.frame.RoiManager;

imp = IJ.getImage();
RoiManager rm = RoiManager.getInstance();
int numRois = rm.getCount();

for(i=0;i<numRois;i++) {
  rm.select(i);
  IJ.run(imp, "Enlarge...", "enlarge=2");
  rm.addRoi(imp.getRoi());
}
```

This snippet shows you some basic scripting to deal with ROIs. We first retrieved an instance of the ROI Manager, which allows us to get the ROIs as an array for processing. In the loop, we selected each ROI and used the enlarge command to increase the size of the ROI by 2 pixels in the *X* and *Y* directions. Finally, we added the enlarged ROIs to the ROI Manager so that we could use them later on if we would like to. This code can be used almost verbatim as Java code. The first error you would receive if you tried to compile it is contained in the following line:

```
imp = IJ.getImage();
```

This works perfectly fine in a BeanShell script, but in an ImageJ plugin, it will generate an error as the type of the `imp` variable is not declared. Also, the for loop does not declare the type for the index `i` iterator, which will also generate a compiler error.

Saving and running your scripts

Once we have created a testable version, we can save it and try running it. Macros are stored with either the `.ijm` or the `.txt` extension. The `.ijm` extension is preferable, as it allows the distinction between regular (non-script) text files and macro files. Script files have their own extensions: `.bsh` for BeanShell and `.js` for JavaScript.

When saving the script, the naming has to adhere to the limitations of the filesystem. Otherwise, there are no specific restrictions for the name. The location to store the scripts by default is the `scripts` or `macros` folder in the ImageJ installation folder, which I will refer to as `$IJ_HOME`. If you wish to run scripts from the command line, it is best to avoid using spaces in the filename to avoid unexpected behavior (that is, if you forget to escape the space character).

> For Fiji, the `$IJ_HOME` folder is called `Fiji.app` and can be placed at any location in the filesystem. It is recommended that you store this folder in your user account's folder, where you have read and write access. On OSX systems, the default location for Fiji is `/Applications/Fiji.app` when using the package installer.

As described about ImageJ macros in the previous chapter, BeanShell and JavaScript scripts can be installed and executed in similar ways. When using Fiji, you can open the scripts in the code editor to run them.

Plugins for ImageJ

As we saw in the previous sections on the BeanShell scripting language, ImageJ provides an easy interface that has access to the full Java API. This also holds true for plugins. Besides the core ImageJ API, plugins can also access the full Java API by importing classes or interfaces in their source files. With the current developments within the ImageJ community, there is a new implementation of the ImageJ core code being developed, called ImageJ2. In the following sections, I will briefly give an overview of some of the changes that will influence the development of plugins. This involves introducing some constructs that are used commonly in larger projects, specifically Git and Maven. Note that knowledge of these constructs is not essential to create plugins, but they will help in creating more consistent and reproducible code. These constructs are also not specific for ImageJ2, but the ImageJ2 project was built up around those concepts. However, I will start by introducing some classes that are specific for ImageJ and deal with handling images and selections.

ImageJ main class

The main ImageJ class refers to the class that gives access to the ImageJ application. We already saw this class in the BeanShell sections earlier. The class is called IJ, which is a static utility class. As shown earlier, this class allows access to the current image as well as other functions. The use of this class is the same as shown earlier, except when writing plugins, you need to explicitly declare the variable type. For instance, when we wish to create a new hyperstack with two 16-bit channels and 10 frames and a size of 512 X 512 pixels, we could use the following code snippet:

```
import ij.IJ;
import ij.ImagePlus;

ImagePlus imp = IJ.createHyperStack("New Stack",512,512,2,1,10,16);
```

Note that we need to specify that the `imp` variable is of type `ImagePlus`, which differs from the scripting languages that we saw earlier. Another useful method of the `IJ` class is the `log()` logging method. This method prints a string to a log window, and displays the log window if it is not open yet. This function is useful for presenting intermediate results or status updates when processing large datasets. To use it, we can just call the method and supply the string we wish to print:

```
IJ.log("We finished processing "+nFiles+" file(s)!");
```

This assumes there is a variable called `nFiles`, which stores the number of files that need to be processed. The log message will tell us how many files were processed, depending on the number of files selected when the plugin was executed. There are also methods to open images or get the active image, which are identical to the examples used in the scripting section (with the only difference that the type needs to be declared explicitly in a plugin).

WindowManager

The `WindowManager` class is a utility class in ImageJ that keeps track of all the windows (including images, results, and log windows), and provides methods that allow the selection of specific windows. Some of the most useful methods are `getImageTitles()`, `getImage()`, and `getCurrentImage()`. The `getImageTitles` method returns a `String` array with all the titles of open images. This function is useful to populate a list of files to allow the user to select a specific image for processing. The following example code will show this functionality and how it can be used within a program:

```
String[] imageList = WindowManager.getImageTitles();

JComboBox jcbImages = new JComboBox(imageList);
```

This is a very user-friendly way of allowing the user to select the image for processing. Normally, ImageJ uses the last open images (the active image) by default. When the user has selected an image based on the title of the image, we can use the `getImage` method to activate that image for further processing:

```
ImagePlus imp;
imp = WindowManager.getImage(imageList[idx]);
```

This allows the rest of the program to use the specified image for processing. This code will be revisited in the chapter on plugins with user interfaces.

ImagePlus

The main class for images is the `ImagePlus` class, which is the main class to deal with images in ImageJ. We already briefly saw the call in the code section earlier. When invoking the `ImagePlus` class, we gain access to several get methods that help with extracting information from the image. We also apply changes to the image using set methods:

```
ImageProcessor ip = imp.getProcessor();
int[] pxVal = imp.getPixel(256,256);
imp.setRoi(256,256,32,32);
```

This snippet shows a few methods that allow you to retrieve aspects of the image as well as set a region in the current image. Another important method that can be accessed using the `ImagePlus` class is the `ImageProcessor` class, as shown in the first line of the code snippet. The next section will deal with this class.

ImageProcessor

The `ImageProcessor` class is a class that allows you to work with the pixel array of an image. There are four different subclasses of the `ImageProcessor` class, which are linked to the different image types: `ByteProcessor` for 8-bit and binary images, `ShortProcessor` for 16-bit images, `FloatProcessor` for 32-bit float images, and `ColorProcessor` for RGBa images. Some of the methods that are accessible from an `ImageProcessor` instance include `autoThreshold()`, `crop()`, `getPixel()`, and `getIntArray()`. These functions allow you to set a threshold on an image, crop the image, retrieve the pixel value at a specified location or get all the pixel values as an array, respectively.

RoiManager

The `RoiManager` class gives the user access to the ROI Manager and all its functions. This class is essential to retrieve and manipulate the regions that were set either manually or programmatically. The `getRoisAsArray()` method allows the user to retrieve all the regions in the ROI Manager as an array, which enables the user to loop over all the regions for measurements or modifications to the regions. The following code is an example:

```
RoiManager rm = RoiManager.getInstance();
if (rm == null) {rm = new RoiManager();}

Roi[] regions;
regions = rm.getRoisAsArray();

for (int r=0; r<regions.length; r++) {
  Roi region;
  region = regions[r];
  //do something...
}
```

It is recommended that you use the `getInstance()` method to get a reference to the ROI Manager. If it returns a null value, you could use the constructor to create a new instance. After using the `getRoisAsArray()` method, you get an array of type `Roi`, which contains a list of regions.

You can also merge the declaration and instantiating of the `regions` variable to a single statement. I prefer to declare my variables at the beginning of a method or class and instantiate them when I have the data available. Declaring a variable before instantiating it would be essential if you need the scope of the variable to extend beyond the point where it is instantiated or assigned. When a variable is used inside and outside of a loop, but the value is only assigned within the loop, the declaration needs to be placed outside of the loop and the assignment within the loop.

The Roi class

The `Roi` class is a generic class that encompasses all the region types that ImageJ supports. You can use this class to retrieve relevant properties of a region, such as the bounding box of the region using the `getBounds()` method. It is also possible to change the size using the `grow()` method. The `Roi` class has several subclasses that are linked to the different region types available in ImageJ. Some of these subclasses have additional methods that are specific for area regions. For instance, the `PolygonRoi` subclass has methods to retrieve the coordinates of the polygon, `getXCoordinates()` and `getYCoordinates()`, which return an `int` array of coordinates.

The Application Programming Interface

As with many programming languages, ImageJ has a well-documented **Application Programming Interface (API)**. It describes all of the classes, methods, and fields that are accessible for programming. The API reference can be found on the ImageJ website at `http://javadoc.imagej.net/ImageJ1` (ImageJ1.x), `http://javadoc.imagej.net/ImageJ` (ImageJ2), and `http://javadoc.imagej.net/Fiji` (Fiji). The API documentation is an efficient way to find classes and methods that can be used to extract relevant information. The classes mentioned in the previous sections can be found using the API page. You can also find a complete list of methods and fields that are available, including the return types of the methods. In the section on setting up an IDE to develop plugins, I will also briefly explain how to set up the generation of Javadoc. Javadoc is a method that parses your source code and extracts specially formatted comments to build up a documentation manual. This can be done for the ImageJ source code, which results in an API that can be accessed offline. I will also show you how to write your own Javadoc documentation and then generate an API for your own code in the chapter on plugin development. This is not essential for small projects, but can be very helpful for large projects with complex code that uses many classes and methods.

Setting up NetBeans IDE

We will now look at how to set up an **Integrated Development Environment** (IDE) that can be used to develop ImageJ as well as plugins for ImageJ. There are many IDEs available for Java. While this section will show you how to set up a specific IDE called NetBeans, many of these settings and configurations can be replicated in your preferred IDE.

The setup I will describe is for the NetBeans IDE, which is developed by the same company that manages the Java language. It can be downloaded in different variants, including a variant for Java development, webpage development, and C++ development. If you only wish to develop plugins for ImageJ, the Java SE (Standard Edition) or Java EE (Enterprise Edition) downloads should be fine. The enterprise edition is similar to the standard edition, but it has additional APIs for multilevel and scalable applications as well as secure network applications. It is possible to extend the basic Java edition and add modules for web development or C++ coding later on using the **Plugins Manager (Tools | Plugins)**.

For the upcoming sections, I will assume that the Java SE was installed. However, to set up the environment, it should not make a difference. It can be downloaded from `https://netbeans.org/downloads/`. After downloading, it can be installed using the standard method for your platform. For Windows systems, there is an installer that can be run by double-clicking. For OS X, there is DMG with a package file that can be used for installation. For Linux systems, there is a shell script installer, and some distributions may supply it from their repositories. It is recommended that you use the version from the NetBeans website, as it is more recent than the version in many of the repositories.

The following sections will describe how to develop ImageJ1.x plugins without using project tools. This method only requires a single download and functions as a standalone development platform. If you wish to develop plugins using the Maven platform for ImageJ1.x and ImageJ2, the following sections can be skipped, and you can continue to the *Developing plugins using Maven* section.

Gathering all components

After the installation has completed, you should be able to launch the NetBeans application. When you launch it for the first time, there will be a start page that allows you to take a tour of the software and watch a quick tutorial project. You can examine the settings and adjust them to your liking.

Next, we need to download the source code for ImageJ. The source code can be downloaded from the ImageJ website at `http://imagej.nih.gov/ij/download/src/`, where you will find a list of different versions, from version 1.20 up to the most recent version (1.50a). Which version you download is not critical. However, it is best to use the most recent version with the recent bug fixes and functionality added. After the download has finished, the archive can be extracted, resulting in a folder named `source`. For the following sections, I will assume that the content of the `source` folder was extracted to the `ij/src` folder within the Documents folder of your user profile. This folder location will be referred to as the `source` folder in the next sections.

Setting up a project

The setup of the project described here follows the description given at `http://rsb.info.nih.gov/ij/developer/NBTutorial.html`, but with a few adjustments. First, the method to create a project does not work properly when using NetBeans version 8.0. The steps described here will accomplish the same result but with a few key changes.

The first step is to set up a new project for ImageJ in NetBeans.

1. To do so, go to **File | New Project…**, which will open the following dialog:

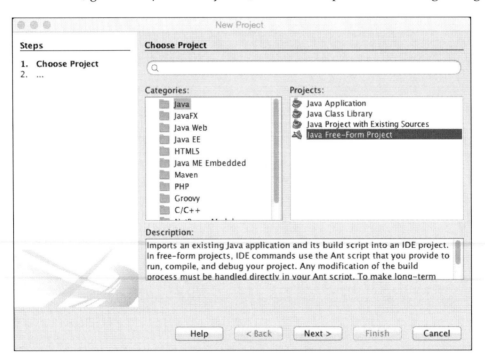

2. In the dialog, select the **Java** category and select **Java Free-Form Project**, as shown in the figure. Then, click on **Next >**.

3. In the next step, we have to select the folder that contains the source. **Click on Browse...** and select the src folder that contains the extracted source code. If the copying was done properly, the remaining fields will be completed automatically with the correct information:

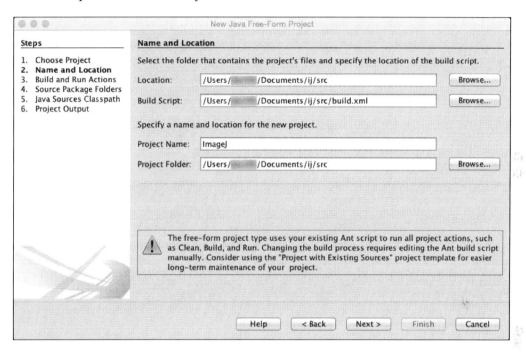

4. We can now click on **Next >** to proceed to **Build and Run Actions** and then click on **Next** again without modifying the fields.

5. In the next step, we have to set the locations that will contain our source code for ImageJ and for our plugins.

6. To do so, add the `ij/src/ij` and `ij/src/plugins` folders in the **Source Package Folders** field. You can remove the first entry marked with a period from the source package folders. I have set the source level to JDK 1.7, which forces NetBeans to use a newer version of Java compared to the definition in the build instructions of the ImageJ source code:

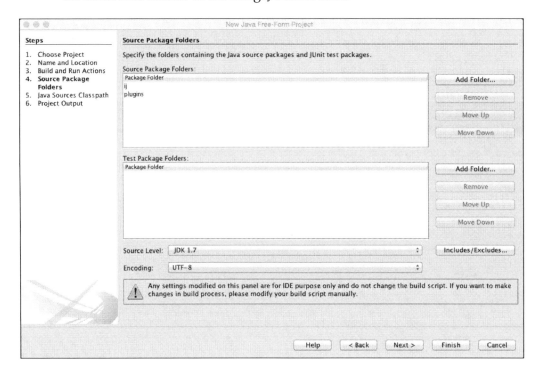

7. Click on **Finish** to complete the setup process:

 The last two steps can be kept to default settings.

The project will now be created, and the main window of NetBeans will show the new project in the **Projects** tab on the left-hand side. The project name (`ImageJ`) has two package sources below it: one for ImageJ source code (`ij`) and one for the plugin source code (`plugins`).

The **Files** tab will show an overview of the files associated with the project:

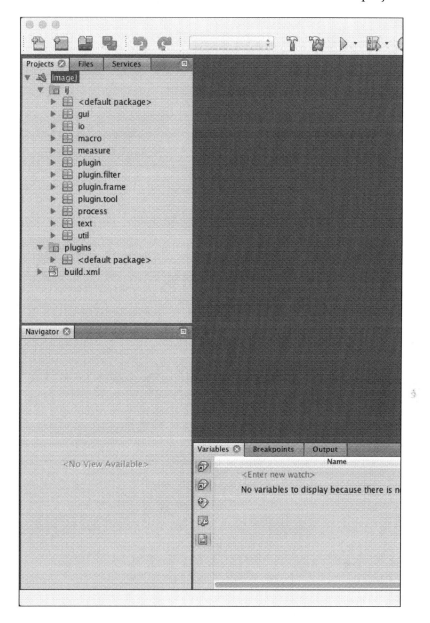

The next section will look at the configuration required building build ImageJ.

Building ImageJ

We will now set up the environment to build ImageJ. This will allow us to create a functional ImageJ program from which we will be able to execute our plugins and macros. The first step is to modify the build instructions that will be used when building the ImageJ project. To do so, select the **Projects** tab and double-click on the `build.xml` file at the bottom of the ImageJ project to open the build file. This is a standard XML file that can be edited using the XML syntax. To disable sections of code, you can use either a comment tag (`<!-- -->`) around that section or delete it completely. The comment method is advised if you wish to restore the file to the original state. The first line that needs to be disabled is line 12 (I'm using comments to disable it):

```
<!-- <exclude name="plugins/**"/> -->
```

Save the file after making the change. Next, we will remove the two `.source` files from the `plugins` folder, but not the `.class` files. We can now start building ImageJ, by clicking on **Run | Build Project (ImageJ)** or pressing *F11*. There may be a few red warnings in the **Build output** window, but these can be ignored for now. At the end of the output, it should say **BUILD SUCCESSFUL**. We will now add the newly created ImageJ build to the project. To do so, go to **File | Project Properties (ImageJ)** and then to the **Java Sources Classpath** category. First, select **ij[ij]** as the source package folder and click on the **Add JAR/Folder** button. Browse to the `src` folder, select the `ij.jar` file, and press the **Choose** button. Repeat this for the `plugins` **[plugins]** source package folder, and then press **OK** to finish. We are now ready to set up the configuration to develop plugins.

Creating a plugin

We will now create a very basic plugin to prepare everything to compile and debug plugins using NetBeans. First, switch to the **Files** tab and right-click on the plugins folder. Then, go to **New | Java Class** from the context menu. In the dialog that opens, set the **Class Name** to `Plugin_Frame` (or something else, but always include an underscore in the name!). It is advised that you create a package for the new class instead of the default package (I'm using **Template** as an example). Click on **Finish** to create the new Java source file:

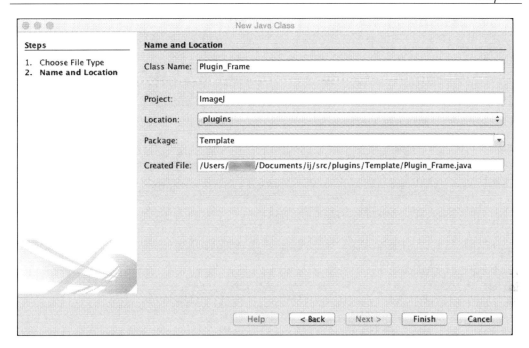

Next, we will place the following code in the newly created source file:

```java
import ij.ImagePlus;
import ij.plugin.filter.PlugInFilter;
import ij.process.ImageProcessor;


public class Plugin_Frame implements PlugInFilter {
  protected ImagePlus imp;

  public int setup(String arg, ImagePlus imp) {
    this.imp = imp;
    return DOES_8G | DOES_16 | DOES_32;
  }

  public void run(ImageProcessor ip) {
    ip.invert();
  }
}
```

This will create a plugin that inverts the LUT of the currently active image. Next, save the source file, and we will compile the code that we just added to our source file. To compile the source code, go to **Run | Compile File** or press *F9*.

A window will pop up to ask whether you wish to generate an ide-file-targets.xml file, so click on **Generate**. A new file will open that contains the build instructions for your plugin:

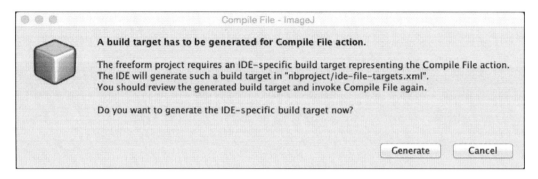

In the `ide-file-targets.xml` file, we will modify two lines. First, we will change line 9 to the following:

```
<javac destdir="plugins" includes="${files}" source="1.7"
srcdir="plugins">
```

We will replace `${build.classes.dir}` with `plugins`. Next, we will comment line 8 (or delete it):

```
<!-- <mkdirdir="${build.classes.dir}"/> -->
```

Now, save the modified file and select your plugin file again. We will compile the file again by going to **Run | Compile File** or by pressing *F9*. In the output view, it should show that the build was successful. Next, we are going to set up the debugging for plugins. Select **Debug | Debug Project (ImageJ)** at which point a dialog will pop up asking for the output to be set. Click on **Set Output** and then on **OK** to accept the default values. Go to **Debug | Debug Project (ImageJ)** again, and NetBeans will ask to generate an `ide-targets.xml` file. Click on **Generate** to create the file and leave the file unaltered. For the final time, go to **Debug | Debug Project (ImageJ)**. This time, ImageJ will launch, and your plugin can be found in the **Plugins** menu. To start your plugin, select **Plugins | Template | Plugin Frame Plugin**, and your plugin should become visible.

Whenever you want to test or change your code, remember to close the ImageJ instance that was created when you select debug. Every time you select **Debug Project (ImageJ)**, a new ImageJ window will open. This will make it very difficult to keep track of which code you are actually debugging.

Creating documentation

The Java language has a nicely integrated way of creating documentation using specially formatted comments within the source files. When applied consistently in your source files, it can be very easy to create an API document. In the next section, we will look at how to set up the basics for documentation.

ImageJ Javadoc

We will first generate the Javadoc for the ImageJ project. To do so, we will select the ImageJ project and go to **Run | Generate Javadoc (ImageJ)**. The Javadoc will be generated for the ImageJ project in a folder named `api`, which can be found in the `/ij` folder. It contains a list of HTML files and style files. To view the documentation, just view the `index.html` file in a web browser, and you will see the ImageJ API documentation. This view is very similar to the API that we saw online in the section on the API, and the information is identical. It is usually not necessary to generate Javadoc for the ImageJ project multiple times, unless you modify the documentation. In the next section, we will look at creating some Javadoc comments for your own plugins.

Plugin Javadoc

To generate Javadoc for your plugins, you need to add some specially formatted comments to your code. There is a lot of documentation about Javadoc online, so the information presented here will be very basic, but should provide a useful starting point. To start with, you first need to decide how much documentation is required. You can make well-crafted documents with a lot of detail, but if your code is very simple, it would cost much more time to write the documentation than to develop the code. That being said, it will be helpful to have some documentation to be able to identify the function that a method serves after some time has passed.

Let's look at an example of documentation for a simple method that has input parameters and an output parameter.

```
private double[] measureParticles(Roi[] r, ImagePlus imp) {}
```

This is the basic method definition of a function to measure some properties of a collection of regions within an image, and it returns an array of measurements. To include the documentation, we will precede the function definition with the following section:

```
/**
 * Take regions within an image and measure the fractal
 * dimension of the provided regions.
 *
 * @param r Roi array containing the particles
 * @param imp reference to image containing the particles
 * @return array with the same dimensions as r containing
 * the values for the fractal dimension.
 */
```

A Javadoc section needs to start with a forward slice followed by two asterisks. When you press enter after the Javadoc opening tag, NetBeans will generate the code for the input parameters (@param) and the return value (@return) automatically. The only thing you have to add is the actual meaning of the parameters.

Once your code has been documented, you will have to instruct NetBeans to build the Javadoc code. To do this, make the following adjustments to the build.xml file by replacing the existing javadoc section (it should be at the end of the file) with the following instructions:

```
<target name="javadocs" description="Build the JavaDocs.">
<delete dir="../plugins_api" />
<mkdir dir="../plugins_api" />
<javadoc
destdir="../plugins_api"
            author="true"
            version="true"
            use="true"
windowtitle="ImageJ plugins API">
<fileset dir="." includes="**/*.java" />
</javadoc>
</target>
```

This will build the ImageJ and your plugins documentation in a folder named `plugins_api`, located one level above your source data. If you created a package for your plugins, you also need to create a `package-info.java` file that contains the information about the package. To create this info file, right-click on your package in the **Projects** view and go to **New | Java Package Info...** from the context menu. Alternatively, you can also go to **New | Other...** in the menu. In the dialog that opens, just click on **OK** to accept the default values. The file will be generated, and you can add your package documentation right above the package line in the usual way. You need to create this info file for every package that you create.

After the documentation is compiled, you can view it by opening the `plugins_api/index.html` file in a browser. The ImageJ documentation will be shown first in the overview panel in the top-left corner. At the bottom will be your package(s). By clicking on them, you will see all the classes that are defined within the package. When you click on a class, the documentation that you supplied will be shown and can be browsed.

Developing plugins using Maven

In the previous sections, I discussed how to set up NetBeans for the development of ImageJ and plugins in a standalone configuration. However, as the design of ImageJ is being expanded, there was a need to create a more modular approach. This approach involves a more project-based building of different modules into a single program. The advantage of such a modular approach makes for a very flexible application that can be expanded in the future. The disadvantage is that it requires a little more overhead to make sure that all dependencies are met for a fully functional program. This is where Apache Maven comes in. Maven is a toolset to describe how to build a project into a finished program and which dependencies are required.

It does this using a special file called the **Project Object Model** (**POM**), which is an XML file. This file is stored in the root of your project and is called `pom.xml`. The content of the file describes some aspects of the project, such as a unique set of identifiers, and a list of dependencies that are required by the project. When you tell Maven to parse the POM file, it will collect all the required resources and compile the source code, run specified tests, and finally package the program in a JAR file. Maven is aimed at taking a clear project description and performing all the required tasks necessary to create the final package automatically without the developer needing to specify each step manually. This is what the previous sections described using the Ant mechanism to build code. First, let's look at how the POM is constructed in Maven, and how it's used to build a project.

Construction of the POM

The POM file describes the structure of a project. It describes the location of the source code (by default, this is `/src/main/java`) and the build directory where the compiled program is stored (by default, this is `/target`). The minimal POM file contains the following structure:

```
<project>
   <modelVersion>4.0.0</modelVersion>
   <groupId>some.packaged.app</groupId>
   <artifactId>my-app-name</artifactId>
   <version>1.0.0</version>
</project>
```

This minimal POM file will inherit all the defaults from the Super POM file. This means, everything that is not explicitly named in the POM; the default values will be used. This includes values such as the location of the source files, the `build` directory, the build file type (`.jar` by default), and other options such as the repositories used to download sources. For an ImageJ1.x plugin, the following POM is the minimal description:

```
<project>
<modelVersion>4.0.0</modelVersion>
<parent>
   <groupId>net.imagej</groupId>
   <artifactId>pom-imagej</artifactId>
   <version>13.2.0</version>
   <relativePath />
</parent>

<groupId>sc.fiji</groupId>
<artifactId>Plugin_Name</artifactId>
<version>1.0.0</version>

<name>plugins/Plugin_Name.jar</name>
<description>A Maven project implementing an ImageJ1.x plugin</
description>

<properties>
   <main-class>Plugin_Name</main-class>
</properties>

<dependencies>
   <dependency>
```

```
        <groupId>net.imagej</groupId>
        <artifactId>ij</artifactId>
    </dependency>
  </dependencies>

  <build>
    <plugins>
      <plugin>
        <artifactId>maven-jar-plugin</artifactId>
        <configuration>
          <archive>
            <manifest>
              <mainClass>${main-class}</mainClass>
            </manifest>
          </archive>
        </configuration>
      </plugin>
    </plugins>
  </build>

  </project>
```

This describes the project using ImageJ as the parent project. This is necessary because the plugin we want to develop requires the ImageJ to be built. Next, we specified the `artifactId` using the name of our plugin; in this case, I used the generic name `Plugin_Name`. In the `properties` field, we stated the main class of the project, which is the name of the plugin.

> Note that the `<version>` tag within the `<parent>` tag will control which version of ImageJ1.x will be retrieved. Using version 7.0.0 will retrieve version 1.49q, while 13.2.0 will retrieve version 1.50a.

Next, we described the dependencies that are required for the plugin, which is ImageJ for a plugin. Finally, we described the build process, stating that we want a JAR file. The manifest should include the `main` class described by the main-class field in the properties object. This method does not require any downloading of source code. The next section will explain how to set up a plugin for ImageJ1.x using a POM in NetBeans.

Creating a Maven plugin project

Using a Maven project to develop a plugin is very simple and only requires a few basic steps. In many cases, you can use the default values from the POM model, and you will only need to specify the name of your plugin(s), a version number, and an artifact name. We will start by creating a new Maven project using NetBeans by going to **File | New Project** from the menu. From the categories list, we will select **Maven**, and from the **Projects** list, we will select **POM Project** and click on **Next >**:

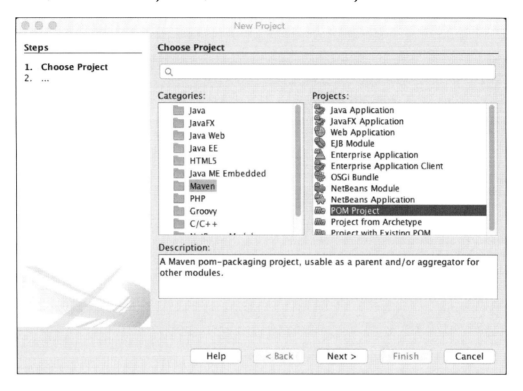

In the next window, we can set the main properties of our plugin. For this example, I will create a dummy plugin that I will call `Awesome_Plugin`. I will place it in the NetBeans workspace folder, which is the default folder that is created when you install NetBeans:

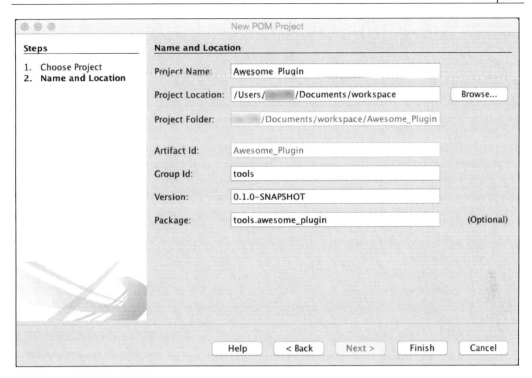

I added **Group ID** and a version number, but these can be changed later on quite easily. After pressing **Finish**, the project will be created and added to your project view (if you cannot see your project view, select **Window | Projects** from the menu). If you expand the project, you will notice that there are three folders, with the most important one, at the moment, being **Project Files**. This folder contains the pom.xml file that we will edit next. You can open the POM file for editing by expanding the project files folder in the project or by right-clicking on the project root and selecting **Open POM** from the context menu. The POM file will now look as follows:

```xml
<?xml version="1.0" encoding="UTF-8"?>
<project xmlns="http://maven.apache.org/POM/4.0.0" xmlns:xsi="http://
www.w3.org/2001/XMLSchema-instance" xsi:schemaLocation="http://maven.
apache.org/POM/4.0.0 http://maven.apache.org/xsd/maven-4.0.0.xsd">
<modelVersion>4.0.0</modelVersion>

<groupId>tools</groupId>
<artifactId>Awesome_Plugin</artifactId>
<version>0.1.0-SNAPSHOT</version>
```

```
<packaging>pom</packaging>

<properties>
<project.build.sourceEncoding>UTF-8</project.build.sourceEncoding>
</properties>

<name>Awesome_Plugin</name>
</project>
```

As you can see, NetBeans added a few more properties to the `<project>` tag, identifying the XML schema that was used for this POM file. It also set the `<properties>` tag with a tag stating the source file encoding that will be used (UTF-8). It also states which packaging will be used. For plugins, we need to change this to JAR. There are two ways to change a parameter in the POM file. The first one is to modify the `pom.xml` file directly by adding or modifying tags. The other option is to select **Properties** from the context menu by right-clicking on the project. This will provide a form that contains many of the fields that are placed in the `pom.xml` file. For the remainder of this section, I will assume we edit the `pom.xml` file directly, as this allows for more flexibility and gives access to more tags than the properties dialog provides.

In order to state that we require ImageJ to be present for our plugin, we will include the `<parent>` tag and its contents, as shown earlier. Next, we will take the `<dependencies>` tag and its contents and add them to the `pom.xml` file. When we now save the `pom.xml` file, you may notice that the folder structure in the project view changes. There are now only two folders called `Dependencies` and `Project Files`. You may also notice that the **Dependencies** folder contains two files: `ij-1.50a.jar` and `tools.jar`. These files are `required` to launch ImageJ. The former file is the actual ImageJ program, while the latter is a jar file that ImageJ requires to run.

If we try to build or run our project at this stage, we will get an error from NetBeans. It is complaining that the project is missing a file to build. This is not surprising as we haven't stated which file we want to build. Also, we haven't defined a main class yet to run, so we first need to fix this issue. To state where our main class will be, we will add the `<main-class>` tag to the `<properties>` tag:

```
<main-class>Awesome_Plugin</main-class>
```

Now that we have stated where our main class will be found, we need to specify how to build the project. We will do this using the `<build>` tag, as shown in the minimal ImageJ POM earlier. The line within the `<manifest>` tag describes that we wish to use the main class defined in the properties described by the `<main-class>` tag:

```
<mainClass>${main-class}</mainClass>
```

After saving the POM file, we can try to build the plugin again, but we will still get an error. This is because we are still missing the actual source code. We have created a project description, but we haven't created a source file yet. We will now add a source file to our project, which must have the same name as the value of the `<artifactId>` tag. To add the source file, right-click on the project in the project view and select **New** | **Java Class**. This will open the **New Java Class** dialog:

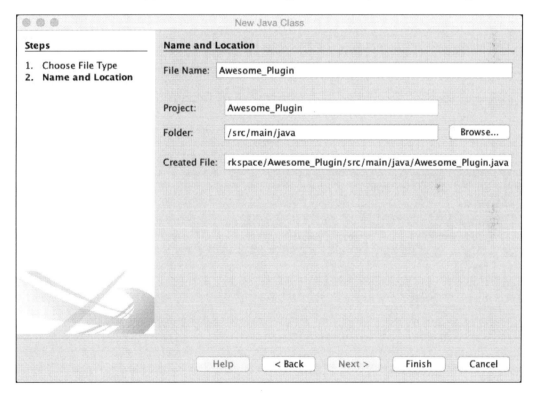

The filename needs to be set to Awesome_Plugin for this example, as this is the artifactId that we used up to now. The folder where we wish to place the file needs to be specified as /src/main/java, as this is the default location used in POM projects. Since I did not change this value, we need to specify it here as well. If you change the location of the source folder, you need to specify it in the new Java class and POM files. After clicking on **Finish**, the file will be created and displayed in your project inside a new folder. The Source Packages folder has been added and contains a package called <default package>, which contains your source file called Awesome_Plugin.java.

 If you wish to place the plugin in a specified package, you can add a package declaration to your source file and ask NetBeans to move the file to the correct folder. The latter can be done after we add the package statement. We can then press *Alt + Enter* while the cursor is on the package statement and select **Move class to correct folder** from the context menu. This example assumes that we kept the default package.

When we now build the project, we will see that the build is successful, meaning that everything is set up correctly for building. However, when we try to run the project, we will need to supply the main class:

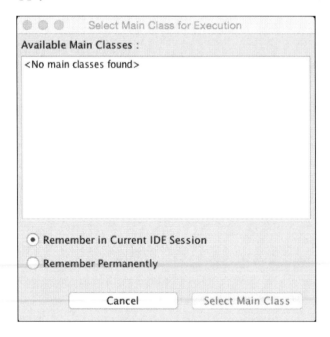

The problem now is that we don't have a main class at this stage. The source code only has a class declaration, but we haven't added any code or a main method. To fix this, we need to add a main method to the source file:

```
public static void main(String[] args) {
   //set the plugins.dir property to make the plugin appear in the
Plugins menu
   Class<?>clazz = Awesome_Plugin.class;
   String url = clazz.getResource("/" + clazz.getName().replace('.',
'/') + ".class").toString();
   int lastIdx = url.lastIndexOf('/');
   String pluginsDir = url.substring(5, lastIdx);
   System.setProperty("plugins.dir", pluginsDir);

   // start ImageJ
   new ImageJ();
}
```

This is a standard main method that is common to Java programs. This method is not required for ImageJ plugins. The standard entry point for plugins is usually the run method (`Plugin` and `PlugInFilter`) or the constructor (`PlugInFrame`). This main method is only for the purpose of the Maven build process and to make sure that ImageJ is started by instantiating a new ImageJ object.

The first line gets a reference to the plugin class that we created. In the next line, we extracted the full path, including the class file. This URL will have the following format: `file:/path/to/Awesome_Plugin.class`. In the next line, we removed the `file:` and the `Awesome_Plugin` parts from the beginning and end of the URL, respectively, using the `lastIndexOf()` method. The `clazz.getName()` call will return a string that will have the following format:

- `class Awesome_Plugin`
- `class package.name.Awesome_Plugin`

The second format would be used if you used a package for your plugin, while the first format is used when you omit the package statement from your plugin. Using the `lastIndexOf()` method, we can include the package folders in the path as well, resulting in an error-free compilation and the correct placement of the plugin in the **Plugins** menu. We will then add the folder that contains the class to the `plugins.dir` property. Finally, we will start ImageJ by invoking a new instance using the `new` keyword.

At this stage, we have the minimal code to run and debug our plugin. When we run the project now, ImageJ should open, and the plugin should be visible in the **Plugins** menu. We can select it, but it may generate an error when we select the plugin from the menu:

This would occur if you used a package definition in your class file (in my example, I used the `analysis.tools` package). You can solve this by adding the following line to the end of your main method:

```
// run the plugin
IJ.runPlugIn(clazz.getName(), "");
```

This will run the plugin immediately after ImageJ has started. If you defined the class without a package statement, you would not encounter this problem. It is, therefore, easier to start by developing plugins using the source files without a package statement. In the upcoming chapters, we will look at what we need to do to make a functional plugin.

Creating an ImageJ2 plugin

The steps to create a Maven project for an ImageJ2 plugin is very similar to the steps taken in the previous section. Only a small change is required in the POM file within the `<dependencies>` tag:

```
<dependencies>
  <dependency>
    <groupId>net.imagej</groupId>
    <artifactId>imagej</artifactId>
  </dependency>
</dependencies>
```

By changing the value of the `<artifactId>` tag from `ij` to `imagej`, we specify that we wish to implement an ImageJ2 instance. When we **Save and Build** the project, we will see that the `imagej-2.0.0-rc-41.jar` file has replaced the earlier `ij-1.50a.jar` file. We would also need the repository for the ImageJ2 project:

```
<repositories>
  <repository>
    <id>imagej.public</id>
    <url>http://maven.imagej.net/content/groups/public</url>
  </repository>
</repositories>
```

The final change that is required is within the plugin source code. We need to use different import statements and change the way ImageJ is launched:

```
import net.imagej.ImageJ;
[...]
public static void main(String[] args) {
  [...]
  // start ImageJ
  final ImageJ ij = net.imagej.Main.launch(args);
}
```

The syntax of ImageJ2 used in plugins is also different compared to ImageJ1.x, which is a topic we will discuss in the following chapters.

Pros and cons of using an IDE

Using an IDE such as NetBeans has some benefits to help you write code. There are options to autocorrect coding errors and the possibility to automatically import dependencies. The disadvantages are not very big, but working with an IDE has a lot of overhead in terms of preparations and setting up. No matter how complete the IDE is, it can still not tell you how to solve a problem. Also, in some cases, it can be faster to just type the code directly using the script editor supplied with Fiji. The IDE is also not well suited to develop ImageJ macros, because macros in ImageJ are not compiled and are, therefore, not easy to integrate in the workflow of the IDE.

Summary

In this chapter, we looked at the framework of macros and plugins that are available in ImageJ. We looked at some of the constructs that the ImageJ API exposes for use in scripting and plugins. Finally, we described how to set up an IDE to develop ImageJ and plugins using it as standalone project or as a Maven-based project. You also saw how to generate documentation using the Javadoc utility.

In the next chapter, we will look at some plugins that are available and how they provide a solution to image-processing problems.

8
Anatomy of ImageJ Plugins

In this chapter, we will examine how a plugin is organized in ImageJ and how it is implemented in the main interface. We will examine both the legacy plugins (ImageJ1.x) and the new format based on SciJava's model (ImageJ2). The following topics will be discussed in this chapter:

- The basic anatomy of a plugin in ImageJ1.x and ImageJ2
- Types of plugins
- Implementing a plugin
- Combining macros and plugins
- Running and debugging plugins
- Examples of available plugins

The basic anatomy of a plugin

A plugin within ImageJ has to adhere to specific rules. The syntax conforms to the Java language, but some of the elements are unique to ImageJ. In the following sections, I will discuss the conventions and constructs used by ImageJ1.x plugins (referred to as **legacy** from here on) and the new SciJav-based conventions and constructs (referred to as **scijava** from here on). Note that when using the scijava model, you are required to use Java 1.7.x or higher when running and compiling your plugins. Also, the scijava model was designed with the Maven and Git systems in mind. This means that it is advantageous to use those systems when developing plugins for the future releases of ImageJ. The following sections will look at the basic anatomy of a plugin in both formats.

Legacy plugins

A plugin within ImageJ1.x has to adhere to specific rules. The syntax conforms to the Java language, but some of the elements are unique to ImageJ. The legacy plugin consists of three main types of plugins: the basic `PlugIn`, `PlugInFilter`, and `PlugInFrame`. A short description and use case for each of these types will follow in the upcoming sections.

The PlugIn type

The `PlugIn` type is used for basic plugins that do not require an image to be open by design. The `PlugIn` type is a Java interface, and it only has one method that needs to be overridden, which is the `run()` method. The `run()` method of the `PlugIn` type is the entry point for this type, and after that, it can be structured in any shape or form using Java syntax. This plugin is very basic, but can perform any task you can design. It can also deal with images. However, selecting an image or opening an image for processing needs to be handled explicitly by the programmer. Also, checking the image type before processing needs to be verified by the programmer explicitly.

The PlugInFilter type

This type of plugin requires an image to be open when the plugin is being executed, and the image also is an input parameter for the plugin. It has two methods that are required to be overridden by the programmer: the `setup()` method and the `run()` method. The setup method does a basic check on the image and allows for the plugin to verify that the current image meets the requirements that are necessary for the processing. It returns an integer value that indicates which types of images can be handled by the plugin. When you wish to specify an image type, you can use the fields defined for the `PlugInFilter` interface:

- `DOES_ALL`: These are any type of image can be processed
- `DOES_8G`: These are the 8-bit gray scale images
- `DOES_16`: These are the 16-bit gray scale images
- `DOES_32`: These are the 32-bit float images
- `DOES_RGB`: These are the RGB images
- `DOES_STACKS`: These are all types of stacks (channels, slices or frames)

When using the DOES_STACKS field, be aware that any multidimensional image will be considered a stack, and processing will run over all the channels, slices, and/ or frames that are present in the image. When using this field, you have to perform checks to make sure that your plugin will process the correct dimension. If the image does not fit the type specified by the field(s), the plugin will abort and give a warning that the image type is not supported by the plugin. If you wish to support different types, you can return the sum of the supported types. The run() method is the main entry point of this type, although you could also perform some preprocessing in the setup method.

The PlugInFrame type

This type of plugin is designed to create an interface for your plugin to show the user. There is no method to be overridden, and the only required element is the constructor for the class. The constructor is the entry point of the plugin. The PlugInFrame type extends the **Abstract Window Toolkit (AWT)** model for the user interface, which can be filled with controls or tabbed panels to allow for a clear user experience. This type does not assume that any images are open, and the developer needs to implement all the logic for the user interface.

Implementing a legacy plugin

Once you have decided on a plugin type, all you need to do is implement your plugin. This sounds simple, and it can be as well. There are a few things you need to consider before you start. ImageJ requires a plugin to have an underscore in the name in order for it to show up in the **Plugins** menu if you use a single class file. This requirement is lifted when you develop the plugin as a **Java archive (JAR)** file. When creating your plugin, you need to adhere to the Java syntax. This means that you need to declare and initialize your variables. When creating functions, you need to specify the return type, if any, and the access type (public/private/protected). The regular coding advice applies to ImageJ plugins as well. Adding comments can be helpful. It is also possible to create documentation for your functions using the Javadoc system that was set up in *Chapter 7, Explanation of ImageJ Constructs*. This allows for a comprehensive documentation of your code, as well as being useful as an extended memory when you need to modify something later on.

When selecting a plugin type, you need to consider certain points. When using PlugInFilter, the active image will be used when the plugin is called, causing the image to be locked by ImageJ. When a command is issued on the image from outside of your plugin, the image is not accessible as it is locked by the plugin. This causes the Image locked error. If you wish to process images using macros from within a plugin, it is better to use the basic PlugIn (or PlugInFrame) type instead of the PlugInFilter type. In the next section, we will look at the constructs for scijava plugins.

Combining macros and legacy plugins

It is possible to combine macros and plugins as well. The run command can be used from within a plugin to execute a specific macro or ImageJ command. The only difference is that you need to precede it with the root class IJ:

```
IJ.run("Green"); //ImageJ command
String status = IJ.runMacro("/PATH/TO/Macro"); //macro
```

The first line will change the lookup table to green for the currently active image and channel. The second line will run a macro specified by a path. The runMacro method returns a string that contains the return value of the macro or NULL if the macro does not return a value. It returns [Aborted] when the macro was aborted or when it encountered an error. The IJ class contains a few useful methods that allow us to run macros and plugins as well as open images using an open dialog. Another useful method is the IJ.log() method, which accepts a string that will be displayed in the log window. This can be used to provide feedback for the user as well as aid in debugging a plugin, as will be shown in a later section. In *Chapter 9, Creating ImageJ Plugins for Analysis* we will look at a basic implementation where we combine ImageJ commands within PlugInFilter.

SciJava plugins

Since ImageJ was developed, many plugins were built using the legacy system described earlier. However, certain shortcomings in the design of the legacy format necessitated a redesign of the ImageJ core. This new framework is the SciJava framework, which consists of scijava-common at its core (among other components). The following sections will describe how plugins are implemented in this new framework. It should be noted that the way plugins are developed in the SciJava framework does not split a plugin in the same types as the legacy system. There is no concept of a plugin that requires an image or that creates a user interface. In the framework, all plugins have the same construction, and they define the components that are required.

The @Plugin annotation

In the SciJava framework, a plugin is a class that is annotated with the @Plugin annotation. Classes with this annotation are automatically recognized by ImageJ and indexed for use when the plugin is launched by the user. Under this framework, you will typically create one of two types of plugins: a service or a command. A service-type plugin will consist of utility methods for internal use in ImageJ. Services provide methods that can be used throughout the framework. Command-type plugins, on the other hand, are meant as plugins that execute a specific function with a specific goal. These are the types of plugins that the user will encounter when using the ImageJ interface: a menu item in ImageJ is a form of a command-type plugin. Command-type plugins can use Service methods to allow for common tasks such as opening images.

Whether you create a command or service-style plugin, either will run in what is called Context. Context in the SciJava framework describes the services and commands that the plugin will use. It functions as a type of sandbox. It is not possible to directly use the methods of services and commands within another plugin's context. If this is required, you have to inject your outside plugin into the context of the plugin of which you wish to use its methods. Alternatively, you can request a service from within a context using a special annotation to request an instance of a type in your plugin using the @Parameter annotation. For instance, if you wish to use logService in your plugin to allow for logging events, you could use the following annotation:

```
@Parameter
private logService logService;
```

When the plugin is run, the context will automatically generate an instance of logService and give you access to its methods:

```
public void log(String msg) {
   logService.info(msg);
}
```

In the upcoming sections, we will look at the two basic types of the @Plugin annotation in more detail.

Services

The SciJava framework contains a large number of generic services that can be used to perform basic tasks and deal with datasets. Some of the more important ones include the following services:

- `AppService`: This deals with applications (that is, ImageJ)
- `EventService`: This deals with events such as mouse clicks
- `PluginService`: This deals with the available plugins and their execution
- `DatasetService`: This deals with tools to handle image data
- `OverlayService`: This deals with tools for overlays and ROIs

To create your own service, you will need to create a context for it and define its methods. If you wish to use the generic services available in the SciJava framework, you can add them as parameters to your own service. This allows for very extensible code that can be reused over and over consistently. In most cases, you will obtain a reference to these services using the `@Parameter` annotation in your plugins, giving you access to its methods and functionality.

Commands

When creating plugins yourself, the command type will be the most commonly used type. Commands describe plugins that face the user and describe an action that the user can perform by launching the command. When creating a plugin, you can specify the type as a `Command` class, and you can specify where the command will be placed in the menu structure:

```
@Plugin(type=Command.class, menuPath="Plugins>My Menu>My Plugin")
public class My_Plugin implements Command {
   //code for the plugin

}
```

The type specifies that this plugin is concerned with a command interface, which it implements as stated in the class definition. The `menuPath` parameter allows you to set the menu position where the plugin will be placed when it is discovered. This allows for fine control and grouping of your plugins. In this case, in a predefined submenu (**My Menu**) within the plugins menu of ImageJ.

Running and debugging plugins

Once you have created your code, you are ready to compile it. Java is not an interpreted language and requires that the source code is compiled into byte code that can be processed by the **Java Virtual Machine** (**JVM**). Depending on how you're developing the code, there are different ways to proceed. You can use ImageJ directly, use the Fiji Code Editor, or use the NetBeans IDE. How you proceed also depends on whether you are developing a legacy plugin or a scijava plugin. The following sections will look at the legacy plugins first.

Compiling plugins

Compiling and running plugins differs a little between vanilla ImageJ and Fiji due to the fact that Fiji is based on the SciJava framework. Also, when using an IDE, there will be different steps involved in compiling and running your plugin.

When you have finished writing the source code for your plugin using vanilla ImageJ, you can run the plugin by first compiling it and then running it. To do so, go to **Plugins | Compile and Run...** and select your plugin. If your code was correctly written, it would compile and then run. If there were any errors during compilation, an error dialog would pop up indicating which line(s) contained error(s). Most of the time, error messages can be very cryptic and may not always point directly to the point where the code failed.

If you are using Fiji, you can compile and run your plugin using the **Run** button at the bottom of the script editor window. The **Compile and Run...** method is not available in Fiji! Any error messages will be displayed in the field below to indicate where and why the compilation or running failed.

If you are using an IDE for your development, you can use the compile function of the IDE. In NetBeans, you can compile your file by going to **Run | Compile File** or by pressing *F9*. If there were no errors during compilation, you can run your plugin using **Run | Run Project** from the menu or by pressing *F6*. If no errors were found, a new instance of ImageJ will be started, and under the **Plugin** menu, your developed plugin should show up. Errors in syntax will prevent the compilation, and the IDE will highlight these errors using a red symbol with a white exclamation mark (as well as a red wavy line):

```
25   public Plugin_Frame() {
26           super("Plugin_Frame");
27           TextArea ta = new TextArea(15, 50);
28           add(ta);
29           pack();
             GUI.center(this);
             show()
32       }
```

When hovering the pointer above the red symbol in the margin, a suggestion is given about the error. In this case, the message tells us that ; was expected at the end of the statement. The symbol above it does not signify an error, but a warning. Warnings will not halt compilation or prevent the running of a plugin. However, they can cause problems during runtime. In this example, the warning tells us that the use of the keyword `this` used in the constructor is not advised and might cause problems. For plugins based on the SciJava framework, the procedures and results are the same. However, there are a few important things to consider. The next section will briefly explain some of the main points.

Compiling SciJava plugins

To compile plugins that implement the SciJava framework, you need to make sure that you have all the dependencies as well as that the ImageJ framework you will run the plugins on supports the framework. For Fiji, this is not a problem. It runs on the framework by default already. You can also use the vanilla ImageJ, but you must make sure it is the ImageJ2 variant and not the **ImageJ1.x** variant.

> You can check which variant you're using by clicking on the status line of the main interface. If it reads something like *ImageJ 2.0.0-[…]*, it indicates you are using ImageJ2. If it reads something similar to **ImageJ 1.50a**, then you are running the **ImageJ1.x** variant.

Due to the modular nature of the framework, it is strongly recommended that you use the Maven tools to create and compile your plugins. This will take care of all the dependencies required to build your plugin. To make this more streamlined and efficient, it is a best practice to use an IDE that supports Maven, although you can also use the **Command-line Interface** (**CLI**) if you wish. To refresh your memory, refer to the previous chapter, which explains you how to set up your IDE with a Maven-based plugin.

To compile your plugin using NetBeans using a Maven-based project, you just need to select your project and go to **Run | Build Project** or press *F11*. To launch your plugin, go to **Run | Run Project** from the menu or press *F6*. Problems that were encountered during compilation will be displayed in a similar way as described for the legacy plugins.

Debugging plugins

As ImageJ is a tool to run the code, it does not have many utilities to debug code. This does not mean, however, that it is not possible to do some debugging. For legacy plugins, you can use the `IJ.log` method. It is possible to log statements to a log window or to look at the value of variables. For plugins built on the SciJava framework, you can use `logService` and use the `info()` and `warn()` methods after declaring `@Parameter` to create an instance to the required service. An example use of this method of debugging plugins can be as follows:

```
int someVar = 1;
int newVar = doSomething(someVar);

//legacy method
IJ.log("Old value: "+someVar+"; New value: "+newVar);

//SciJava method
logService.info("Old value: "+someVar+"; New value: "+newVar);
```

When using this type of method, it can be useful to include a simple control statement such as the `if` statement. This allows you to easily disable or control the amount of logging that is done in your final incarnation of the plugin. Using a global variable that sets a debugging level, you can control to show a certain log message or not:

```
private static int dbglvl = 3;
...

//implement the logging based on the dbglvl value
if (dbglvl> 2) {
  IJ.log("The current value is "+currValue);
}
...
//implement the logging based on the dbglvl value
if (dbglvl> 4) {
  IJ.log("This statement was evaluated...");
}
```

In this case, the global variable dbglvl will dictate which messages will be shown. The first if statement will be executed with the current debug level (set to 3), while the second statement will not be displayed with the current level. In the final version of your plugin, you can change the value of dbglvl to 1 or 0 to disable all low-level debugging statements. Note that this assumes that a high value for dbglvl is associated with minor logging statements, and a low value will only show the most minimal statements. Finally, you might want to remove all the if statements when the code is working correctly. The evaluation of each statement does require a finite amount of time, so it will slow down your code in the end.

When using the NetBeans IDE to develop plugins, there are more options to debug and profile your code. The advantage of using an IDE such as NetBeans is you can set breakpoints where you wish to halt the execution of the plugin and look at the contents of the variables. To do so, click on the margin before the line where you wish to stop. A red square will be displayed, indicating a breakpoint:

```
25      public Plugin_Frame() {
26              super("Plugin_Frame");
27              TextArea ta = new TextArea(15, 50);
                add(ta);
29              pack();
                GUI.center(this);
31              show();
32      }
33
```

The entire line is also colored red to indicate the line where the debugger will wait when you run it. Keep in mind that if you place a breakpoint in a statement that will never be executed, the debugger will never stop, and your code will run uninterrupted.

To run the code using the debugger, you can go to **Debug | Debug Project (...)** or press *Ctrl + F5* on the keyboard. When the debugger hits a breakpoint, the line will become green, and you can continue using the different step functions. In the variables tab at the bottom of the IDE, you will see all the variables that are available at the current breakpoint. Note that you can also evaluate expressions and change the values that are currently assigned to variables. Doing this may cause problems or may lead to infinite loops or crashes, so be careful when changing values!

There is also a profiler to help with identifying sections of code that are not efficient in terms of processing speed or memory usage. However, many of these advanced features are not always necessary when developing simple plugins. Once you start Profiler by selecting **Profile | Profile Project (...)**, you can select whether you wish to monitor the CPU processing, **garbage collection** (**GC**) and/or memory usage. You can use the telemetry to see whether there are problems with excessive CPU cycles as well as problems with garbage collection and memory management. The use of Profiler extends a little too far beyond the scope of this book. However, there are excellent resources available online on how to use and interpret the results from profiling.

As profiling an application is very close to an art form, use it carefully and only when you really notice very slow performance or memory problems in your application. Choosing how much development overhead you wish to dedicate for your plugin should always be weighed against the amount of time it gains. Spending hours of optimizing your code or algorithm so that it executes 1 second faster may not be worth it if it is called only once and is a part of a larger chain of commands. However, if you optimize code that is called hundreds of time within a loop, the optimization might be worth the extra development time many times over.

In the upcoming section, we will look at some plugins that are available and are used for scientific research.

Examples of available plugins

In this section, I will discuss a few plugins that are available for ImageJ, most of which have also been published in scientific journals. They will show you how to use ImageJ for advanced image processing, with different degrees of automation and user interaction. They also provide a few examples of the design of a plugin, either with its own interface or just as a single command that executes. Some of these examples also have their source code available so that you can see how the developers implemented their algorithms. Be aware that having the source code and being able to understand it fully might be difficult: depending on the level of documentation or comments in the code. It might be very difficult to completely retrace the functioning of the code. As a program grows and new functions and algorithms are added, it deviates more from a single core algorithm to a more convoluted group of files. Developers using the Javadoc capabilities available in IDEs can create detailed documentation relatively easy, making the understanding of code slightly easier.

One point that is very important when trying to analyze source code is to realize which file or function is the entry point of the program. You can be sure that when the code executes, it will always go into this main entry point, and every user interaction or function will be set up in the main entry point. The entry points for the different types of plugins were indicated in the previous sections. Also, plugins developed using the SciJava framework generally have a `main()` method, which is not necessarily the entry point for the plugin. This depends on the way that the plugin was launched. When launched through the IDE using Maven, the `main()` method is used to instantiate ImageJ and launch the plugin. However, when launching the plugin from the ImageJ instance using the menu for example, the `main()` method will not be invoked.

When using an interface for your plugin, a lot of the action comes from the user pressing a button, adding a number to a field or selecting an option. The `main` interface just waits for the user to do something. In Java, this means that the `ActionPerformed()` method becomes the entry point for many algorithms or processing. When a user clicks a button, this will fire an action event that can be used by the programmer to catch it and connect it to further statements. First, we will look at some examples of plugins that are available on the ImageJ website (`http://imagej.nih.gov/ij/plugins/index.html`) to show how to develop ImageJ solutions to image processing problems.

Example plugins available in ImageJ and Fiji

ImageJ has a large collection of plugins available that extend the core functionality. With the arrival of ImageJ2, the model for distribution of plugins is changing as well. In the older ImageJ1.x framework, you were required to download a source file of a plugin or a compiled .class file and place it in the plugins folder. When the plugin was updated, you would need to repeat the whole process again. With ImageJ2, an updating mechanism has been provided that uses a repository system. In this system, communication between ImageJ and the repository will determine whether there are updates available. When there are updates, the user can automatically install the updates without having to search for the plugin.

For most of the plugins that are available, the source code can be viewed or studied to look at the way other people have solved a particular image-processing problem. For the following example plugins, I will describe the specific problem or challenge they are designed to tackle. I will then show a bit of code to explain how the plugin tries to solve the problem. Feel free to view or download the source code where available to look at the complete implementation.

MultipleKymograph

An example of such a plugin is the **MultipleKymograph** plugin
(MultipleKymograph_.java), which creates a kymograph along a (segmented)
line selection. It was designed by Jens Rietdorf and Arne Seitz from the **European
Molecular Biology Laboratory** (**EMBL**) in Heidelberg, Germany. It contains a small
set of tools and macros that can be used to create and measure kymographs. We
already saw kymographs back in *Chapter 5, Basic Measurements with ImageJ*, where
we saw how they visualized dynamics in time series. There, we used the **Reslice**
command to generate the kymograph, which worked OK, but there are a few small
drawbacks of that method.

The first problem is that **Reslice** only considers the pixels that are on the line that
was selected. This makes it more sensitive to inaccurate placement of the line and
pixel noise. The **MultipleKymograph** plugin is a legacy plugin that tries to solve this
problem by providing the user with an input field to ask for the line width to be used
to create the averaged output pixels. When the user calls the plugin without a line
selection or an open image, it generates an error message indicating that action needs
to be taken by the user before calling the plugin. As the creation of the kymograph
image itself hinges on the correct values for the pixels, I will focus on how the plugin
calculates the average pixel intensity for the line that was placed by the user.

The main generation of the pixel values happens in the sKymo (...) method, which has
the following definition:

```
public double[] sKymo(ImagePlus imp, ImageProcesso rip, Roi roi, int
linewidth, int proflength){

  int numStacks=imp.getStackSize();
  int dimension = proflength*numStacks;
  double[] sum = new double [dimension];

  int roiType = roi.getType();
  int shift=0;
  int count=0;

  for (int i=1; i<=numStacks; i++) {
    imp.setSlice(i);

    for (int ii=0;ii<linewidth;ii++){
      shift=(-1*(linewidth-1)/2)+ii;

      if (roiType==Roi.LINE) {
        profile = getProfile(roi,ip,shift);
      }
```

```
      else {
        profile = getIrregularProfile(roi, ip,shift);
      }
      for (int j=0;j<proflength;j++){
        count = (i-1)*proflength+j;
        sum[count]+=(profile[j]/linewidth);
      }
    }
  }
  return sum;
}
```

The sum variable that is returned contains the result of the averaged profiles along the stack. The method requires five input parameters, which are as follows:

- ImagePlus imp: This is the source stack that we want to use for the calculations

- ImageProcessor ip: This is the image processor to access the pixels of the stack

- Roi roi: This is the ROI that marks the line we wish to make into a kymograph

- int linewidth: This is the width of the line as specified by the user input

- int proflength: This is the length of the line specified by the user

The method starts by declaring the parameters that will be needed for processing. Specifically, the output variable sum is defined as a double[] vector with a length equal to length of the line multiplied with the number of slices (or frames). The method then iterates over the slices in the stack (the outer for loop) and retrieves the profile using a method called getProfile() or getIrregularProfile(). These methods extract the pixel values from the selection, where the shift parameter determines how far the line is shifted compared to the selection. The only difference between the two is that one is meant to be used for straight lines (getProfile), while the other is used for segmented lines (getIrregularProfile). For the sake of brevity, I will only show the code for the former method:

```
double[] getProfile(Roi roi,ImageProcessor ip, int shift){
  double[] values;

  int x1=((Line)roi).x1;
  int x2=((Line)roi).x2;
  int y1=((Line)roi).y1;
  int y2=((Line)roi).y2;
```

```
    ((Line)roi).x1=x1+shift;
    ((Line)roi).x2=x2+shift;
    ((Line)roi).y1=y1+shift;
    ((Line)roi).y2=y2+shift;

    values=((Line)roi).getPixels();
    ((Line)roi).x1=x1;
    ((Line)roi).x2=x2;
    ((Line)roi).y1=y1;
    ((Line)roi).y2=y2;

    return values;
}
```

This method takes the ROI that the user specified and shifts it by the amount specified in the `shift` parameter. It then uses the `getPixels()` method from the `Roi` class to extract the gray values and returns them. As a line is defined by only two points, each with an *x* and *y* coordinate, this method is fairly brief. The irregular case requires that the line is moved along all the *N* coordinates required to define the segmented line. Otherwise, it functions in the same way.

ColorTransformer2

This legacy plugin is useful when dealing with color images such as those acquired by digital color cameras or videos from cameras such as webcams. It was originally developed by Maria E. Barilla as **ColorTransformer** and modified by Russel Cottrell, resulting in the **ColorTransformer2** plugin. The source code can be found at `http://www.russellcottrell.com/photo/downloads/Color_Transformer_2.java`.

A problem with color images, such as RGB images, is that the intensity is not well-defined in the RGB color space. Light blue might appear more intense than dark blue, but the intensity value for the blue channel might be higher for dark blue than for light blue. In order to segment RGB images effectively based on specific colors, it is better that you transform it to a color space that is more suited for this purpose. The HSB color space separates an image in three components: **Hue**, **Saturation**, and **Brightness** (sometimes also labeled as **Value** or **Intensity**). The hue indicates the color ranging from red to orange, yellow, green, cyan, blue, and magenta. See *Chapter 2, Basic Image Processing with ImageJ* for details on the use of the HSB color space.

This plugin implements a `PlugInFilter`, meaning that it overrides the `setup()` and `run()` methods, which form the entry points for the plugin. The setup method checks whether an image is open and screens the type of image that this plugin can process. The run method shows a dialog, which allows the user to choose the color space to convert from and to. The method I want to describe here is the conversion from RGB to HSI, which is a common format to use in segmentation of RGB images where segmentation needs to be performed based on color.

The main method that performs the actual RGB-to-HSI conversion is the `getHSI()` method. This method looks as follows:

```
public void getHSI(){
  for(int q=0; q<size; q++){
    float var_Min = Math.min(rf[q], gf[q]); //Min. value of RGB
    var_Min = Math.min(var_Min, bf[q]);
    float var_Max = Math.max(rf[q], gf[q]); //Max. value of RGB
    var_Max = Math.max(var_Max, bf[q]);
    float del_Max = var_Max - var_Min;       //Delta RGB value

    c3[q] =  (rf[q] + gf[q] + bf[q])/3f;

    if ( del_Max == 0f ){ //This is a gray, no chroma...
      c1[q] =  0f; //HSL results = 0 ? 1
      c2[q] =  0f;
    }
    else{//Chromatic data...
      c2[q] = 1 - (var_Min / c3[q]);

      float del_R = (((var_Max-rf[q])/6f)+(del_Max/2f))/del_Max;
      float del_G = (((var_Max-gf[q])/6f)+(del_Max/2f))/del_Max;
      float del_B = (((var_Max-bf[q])/6f)+(del_Max/2f))/del_Max;

      if(rf[q] == var_Max) c1[q] = del_B - del_G;
      else if(gf[q] == var_Max) c1[q] = (1f/3f)+del_R-del_B;
      else if(bf[q] == var_Max) c1[q] = (2f/3f)+del_G-del_R;

      if (c1[q] < 0)  c1[q] += 1;
      if (c1[q] > 1)  c1[q] -= 1;
    }
  }
}
```

These conversions are based on the methodology described in *Color Vision and Colorimetry, Theory and Applications, D Malacara*. The transformation is based on transforming the original RGB values stored in the `rf`, `gf`, and `bf` arrays, respectively. The transformed values are stored in the `c1`, `c2`, `c3`, and optionally, `c4` arrays. For the transformation to HSI, the `c4` array is not used, as an HSI image only has three channels. For example, the CMYK color space requires all four channels. At the end of the run method, the values for the channels are placed in a new image, which will be the transformed image.

MtrackJ

This plugin is useful when you wish to track objects over time and, optionally, in three dimensions. It was developed by Eric Meijering at the University of Lausanne in Switzerland. The source code can be found on GitHub at `https://github.com/fiji/MTrackJ/`. It was published in *Methods in Enzymology, vol 504* in February 2012. The main interface of the plugin consists of groups of buttons that allow you to add, delete, or move tracks or points and perform measurements or change settings:

MTrackJ	
Clear	Load
Import	Save
Add	Cluster
Hide	Color
Delete	Move
Merge	Split
Refer	ID
Measure	Movie
Tracking	Displaying
Options	Help

The function of this plugin is to track objects or particles over time in order to establish their speed and direction. Although automated tracking algorithms do exist, some data is just too difficult or too dense for automated tracking algorithms to cope with. For these types of challenges, this plugin will provide a tool that can help establish useful parameters for objects. The goal of this plugin is similar to that of the **MultipleKymograph** plugin described earlier: measuring the velocity of multiple objects. When the tracks are created and measured, the results are presented in a results window. These results can then be used for direct plotting and analysis outside of ImageJ or as input for more advanced analysis.

As this plugin is quite extensive and has many features, I will focus on one very tiny detail that makes this interface great to track objects with amazing accuracy. In the options for tracking, accessed through the **Tracking** button, you can set a snapping function for the mouse cursor. This type of feature might be familiar to many people. Many different applications use it to make it easier to align objects nice and evenly. When you check the **Apply local cursor snapping during tracking** checkbox, you can choose a snap feature. This snap feature will determine when you position your mouse cursor over an object where the tracking point will be added. Without snapping, it would be placed at the pixel that you clicked. However, when using **bright centroid** as the snap feature, something interesting will happen (when using fluorescent images). When you add a tracking point by clicking, **MtrackJ** determines the centroid of the snap range that you defined. The centroid is the weighted intensity point and is not necessarily a single pixel, but it can be a position such as ($x = 12.4$, $y = 13.45$). For image data with good signal-to-noise ratio, you can achieve better tracking resolution than the optical system can provide (so-called subpixel resolution). The location of the snap coordinates are calculated in a method called snapcoords(). I will not reproduce the entire method as it is quite extensive, but I will show you how it achieves the bright centroid calculation:

```
double ox=0, oy=0;
switch (settings.snapfeature) {

    //other cases skipped

  case MTJSettings.BRIGHT_CENTROID: {
    // Make all weights > 0:
    if (minval<= 0) {
      final double offset = -minval + 1;
      for (int y=0; y<snaprect.height; ++y)
        for (int x=0; x<snaprect.width; ++x)
          snaproi[y][x] += offset;
      minval += offset;
      maxval += offset;
    }
```

```
        // Calculate Otsu threshold:
        double otsu = minval;
        final double maxi = OTSU_BINS;
        final double range = maxval - minval;
        double maxvari = -Double.MAX_VALUE;
        for (int i=1; i<OTSU_BINS; ++i) {
          double sum1=0, sum2=0, n1=0, n2=0;
          final double thres = minval + (i/maxi)*range;
          // Notice that we always have minval<thres<maxval,
          // so sum1, sum2, n1, n2 are > 0 after the loop:
          for (int y=0; y<snaprect.height; ++y)
          for (int x=0; x<snaprect.width; ++x) {
            final double val = snaproi[y][x];
            if (val<thres) { ++n1; sum1 += val; }
            else { ++n2; sum2 += val; }
          }
          final double mean1 = sum1/n1;
          final double mean2 = sum2/n2;
          final double vari = n1*n2*(mean1-mean2)*(mean1-mean2);
          if (vari > maxvari) {
            maxvari = vari;
            otsu = thres;
          }
        }
        // Calculate centroid >= threshold:
        double val=0, sum=0;
        for (int y=0; y<snaprect.height; ++y)
        for (int x=0; x<snaprect.width; ++x) {
          val = snaproi[y][x];
          if (val>= otsu) {
            val -= otsu;
            ox += x*val;
            oy += y*val;
            sum += val;
          }
        }
        ox /= sum; // sum can never be 0
        oy /= sum;
        break;
      }
    }
    snapos.x = snaprect.x + ox;
    snapos.y = snaprect.y + oy;
```

As the plugin supports multiple methods for snapping, there are multiple cases in this `switch` statement, which I omitted for the sake of brevity. The goal of the method is to assign values to the `snapos.x` and `snapos.y` variables. For the bright centroid method, a threshold is used based on the **Otsu** method. In the first loop using the x and y indices, we went over the pixels of the snapping rectangle and sum all the pixel intensities (`val`) that are above the threshold value (`thres`) in `sum2` and the intensities below the threshold in `sum1`. We used these to calculate the variation, and if it exceeds the maximum value in the rectangle, we adjust the value and the Otsu threshold value.

In the second loop over the pixels in the snapping rectangle, the centroid is determined by summing the products of each pixel's x and y coordinates multiplied by the intensity above the Otsu threshold. A running sum of the intensities above the threshold is also kept and used to divide the final coordinates with. These final values are used in the `draw()` method function that shows the bright centroid in the image:

```
public void draw(final Graphics g) { try {

    if (!(g instanceofGraphics2D)) return;
    final Graphics2D g2d = (Graphics2D)g;

    //some code skipped for brevity...

    // Draw snapping objects:
    if (snapping()) {
      g2d.setColor(settings.hilicolor);
      try { g2d.setComposite(settings.snapopacity); } catch
      (Throwable e) { }
      // Snap ROI:
      g2d.setStroke(settings.snapstroke);
      final int slx = (int)((snaprect.x-vof.x + 0.5)*mag);
      final int sly = (int)((snaprect.y-vof.y + 0.5)*mag);
      final int sux = (int)((snaprect.x+snaprect.width-vof.x-0.5)*mag);
      final int suy = (int)((snaprect.y+snaprect.height-vof.y-0.5)*mag);
      g2d.drawLine(slx,sly,sux,sly);
      g2d.drawLine(sux,sly,sux,suy);
      g2d.drawLine(sux,suy,slx,suy);
      g2d.drawLine(slx,suy,slx,sly);
      // Snap cursor:
      g2d.setStroke(settings.pointstroke);
      final int xi = (int)((snapos.x - vof.x + 0.5)*mag);
      final int suy = (int)((snapos.y - vof.y + 0.5)*mag);
      final int hps = 6;
```

```
        g2d.drawLine(xi,yi-hps,xi,yi+hps);
        g2d.drawLine(xi-hps,yi,xi+hps,yi);
    }
}
```

This method uses a `Graphics2D` object referenced by `g2d` to create a square box indicating the snap region (the `// Snap ROI` section), whose size is determined by the values of the `snaprect` object. Finally, it draws a small + to indicate the snap coordinate defined by the `snapos.x` and `snapos.y` variables (the `// Snap cursor` section).

Coloc2

For certain types of research questions, it is important to know whether two objects overlap or colocalize. The **Coloc2** is a plugin included in the `Colocalisation_Analysis.jar` file as developed by Daniel J. White, Tom Kazimiers, and Johannes Schindelin. The source is available on GitHub at `https://github.com/fiji/Colocalisation_Analysis/`. The Coloc2 command is used to measure colocalization between two images, usually representing different channels in fluorescent images.

The main functionality is placed in the `colocalise` method, which compares the pixel intensities between the two images using different methods. As an example of how this plugin functions, I will look at a more basic function that is used whenever a selection is present in the ROI manager and needs to be used for the colocalization analysis. The method is called `createMasksFromRoiManager`, and it calls a second method called `createMasksAndRois`:

```
protected boolean createMasksFromRoiManager(int width, int height) {
    RoiManager roiManager = RoiManager.getInstance();
    if (roiManager == null) {
        IJ.error("Could not get ROI Manager instance.");
        return false;
    }
    Roi[] selectedRois = roiManager.getSelectedRoisAsArray();
    // create the ROIs
    createMasksAndRois(selectedRois, width, height);
    return true;
}

protected void createMasksAndRois(Roi[] rois, int width, int height) {
    // create empty list
    masks.clear();
```

```
   for (Roi r : rois ){
     MaskInfo mi = new MaskInfo();
     // add it to the list of masks/ROIs
     masks.add(mi);
     // get the ROIs/masks bounding box
     Rectangle rect = r.getBounds();
     mi.roi = new BoundingBox(
     new long[] {rect.x, rect.y} ,
     new long[] {rect.width, rect.height});
     ImageProcessor ipMask = r.getMask();
     // check if we got a regular ROI and return if so
     if (ipMask == null) {
       continue;
     }

     // create a mask processor of the same size as a slice
     ImageProcessor ipSlice = ipMask.createProcessor(width, height);
     // fill the new slice with black
     ipSlice.setValue(0.0);
     ipSlice.fill();
     // position the mask on the new  mask processor
     ipSlice.copyBits(ipMask, (int)mi.roi.offset[0],
     (int)mi.roi.offset[1], Blitter.COPY);
     // create an Image<T> out of it
     ImagePlus maskImp = new ImagePlus("Mask", ipSlice);
     // and remember it and the masks bounding box
     mi.mask = ImagePlusAdapter.<T>wrap( maskImp );
   }
 }
```

The first step is to retrieve the ROIs from the manager using the
`getSelectedRoisAsArray()` method, which then passes the ROIs to the
`createMasksAndRois` method. This method stores the regions in the `mi.mask`
variable where it can be used by the `colocalise` method. This plugin uses some
constructs derived from ImageJ2. The `ImagePlusAdapter` is a wrapper function from
the `ImgLib2` library. This convenience method allows ImageJ1.x images to be placed
inside an `ImgLib2` container as used by ImageJ2. These functions are essential during
the transition between ImageJ1.x and ImageJ2 and allow for interoperability. Next, I
will take a look at a plugin that was developed within the SciJava framework using
the annotations and the **Command and Service framework** specifically for ImageJ2.

Goutte_pendante

The **Goutte_pendante** plugin (pendant drop) is a plugin built under the SciJava framework by Adrian Daerr at the Université Paris Diderot. The source code can be found on GitHub at `https://github.com/adaerr/pendent-drop`. This project is written using the Maven system, so I will briefly show the `pom.xml` file as an example of how to define a plugin within the framework:

```xml
<?xml version="1.0" encoding="UTF-8"?>
<project xmlns="http://maven.apache.org/POM/4.0.0" xmlns:xsi="http://
www.w3.org/2001/XMLSchema-instance" xsi:schemaLocation="http://maven.
apache.org/POM/4.0.0   http://maven.apache.org/xsd/maven-4.0.0.xsd">
  <modelVersion>4.0.0</modelVersion>
  <parent>
    <groupId>net.imagej</groupId>
    <artifactId>pom-imagej</artifactId>
    <version>7.1.0</version>
    <relativePath />
  </parent>
  <groupId>name.adriandaerr.imagejplugins.pendentdrop</groupId>
  <artifactId>pendent_drop</artifactId>
  <version>2.0.1</version>
  <name>Pendent Drop ImageJ Plugin</name>
  <description>Surface tension measurement through the pendent
    drop method.</description>
  <properties>
    <main-class>Goutte_Pendante</main-class>
  </properties>
  <repositories>
    <repository>
      <id>imagej.public</id>
      <url>http://maven.imagej.net/content/groups/public</url>
    </repository>
  </repositories>
  <dependencies>
    <dependency>
      <groupId>net.imagej</groupId>
      <artifactId>imagej</artifactId>
    </dependency>
  </dependencies>
</project>
```

You can see that the project description is very simple using the POM model. The <parent> tag describes that this utilizes ImageJ. The dependencies state that the ImageJ2 code base should be used, as identified by the <artifactId> tag using imagej instead of ij for ImageJ1.x plugins. Plugins built for ImageJ2 also tend to have a main method. To illustrate its function, I will highlight some of the code from this plugins' main method:

```
public static void main(final String... args) throws Exception {
    final String testImagePath =
    "/home/adrian/Programmes/plugins_ImageJ_src/Traitement_Gouttes/src
    /test/resources/eauContrasteMaxStack.tif";

    // Launch ImageJ as usual.
    //final ImageJ ij = net.imagej.Main.launch(args);
    final ImageJ ij = new ImageJ();
    ij.ui().showUI();

    // Open test image.
    final ServiceHelper sh = new ServiceHelper(ij.getContext());
    final IOService io = sh.loadService(DefaultIOService.class);
    final Dataset dataset = (Dataset) io.open(testImagePath);

    // create a display for the dataset
    final ImageDisplay imageDisplay =
    (ImageDisplay) ij.display().createDisplay(dataset);

    // create a rectangle
    final RectangleOverlay rectangle = new
    RectangleOverlay(ij.getContext());
    rectangle.setOrigin(110, 0);
    rectangle.setOrigin(60, 1);
    rectangle.setExtent(340, 0);
    rectangle.setExtent(420, 1);
    rectangle.setLineColor(Colors.HONEYDEW);
    rectangle.setLineWidth(1);

    // add the overlays to the display
    final List<Overlay> overlays = new ArrayList<Overlay>();
    overlays.add(rectangle);
    ij.overlay().addOverlays(imageDisplay, overlays);
    for (final net.imagej.display.DataView view : imageDisplay) {
      if (view instanceofnet.imagej.display.OverlayView) {
        view.setSelected(true);
      }
```

```
    }

    // display the dataset
    ij.ui().show(imageDisplay);

    // Launch the "CommandWithPreview" command.
    ij.command().run(Goutte_pendante.class, true);
  }
```

This code is only used when testing the plugin and performs a few steps that are useful when testing code but not when actually using the plugin outside of the testing phase. It starts by defining a test image with a hard-coded path string. It then performs the step that all plugins for ImageJ will perform in their main method: launching an instance of ImageJ. It then goes on to open the image specified by the string using IOService and finally displaying it using the ImageDisplay service. The result of this process is the image of a drop hanging from an aperture:

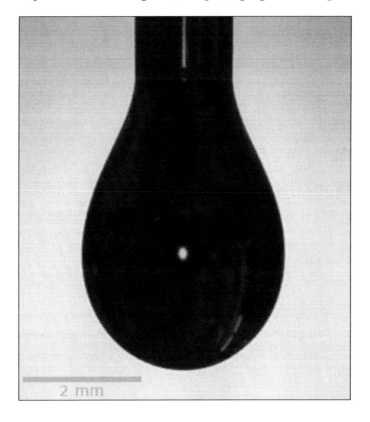

Next, a `rectangle` object is generated over the drop image that was opened. This image will be used as an initial search space for the plugin to detect the drop. This is done using the `RectangleOverlay` class in the `net.imagej.overlay` package. Finally, it adds the overlay to the display and displays the image before calling the plugin in the last statement of the method:

```
ij.command().run(Goutte_pendante.class, true);
```

The used pattern in this plugin is similar to that described in the previous chapter. However, there are additional steps inserted here to make sure that the plugin works fast and correctly. If you would install the plugin using **Update site** through Fiji and try to run it immediately by selecting **Plugins | Drop Analysis | Pendant Drop** from the menu, you will get an error message. This error message states that there is an error executing the `Goutte_pendante#paramInitializer` method. If you run **Plugins | Drop Analysis | About Pendant Drop**, you will see a brief explanation and a usage section for the plugin. In the usage section, there will be an explanation of why it failed. There was no rectangular ROI or image when you launched it. At the bottom of the about dialog, there are buttons with information and documentation, as well as a way to retrieve the image of the drop (bottom button).

The goal of this plugin is to fit the shape of the drop, and the parameters of that fit can be used to say something about the surface tension of the liquid. To do so, it needs a class that describes the shape of the drop that is defined as an object called `Contour` within the plugin. It needs to fit a polynomial to the drop shape in order to determine `Contour` parameters. To do so, it is necessary to determine the borders of the drop. This is achieved by a method called `findDropBorders()`. This function will find the shoulders of the drop and store the locations in arrays for the left and right borders:

```
private boolean findDropBorders(ImageProcessor ip) {
  leftBorder = null;
  rightBorder = null;

  for (int y = bounds.height - 1; y >= 0; y--) {

    // find border positions with integer precision
    // left border first
    int xl = 0;
    while (xl <bounds.width &&
      ip.getPixelValue(bounds.x + xl, bounds.y + y) > threshold)
    xl ++;

    if (xl >= bounds.width) {// drop not detected in this scanline
      if (leftBorder != null) {
```

```
         leftBorder[y]  = Double.NaN;
         rightBorder[y] = Double.NaN;
      }
      continue;
   } else if (leftBorder == null) {
      // allocate array on drop tip detection
      leftBorder = new double[y+1];
      rightBorder = new double[y+1];
   }

   // right border next
   int xr = bounds.width - 1;
   while (xr> xl &&
      ip.getPixelValue(bounds.x + xr, bounds.y + y) > threshold)
   xr --;
   xr ++; // so xl and xr point just to the right of the interface

   // don't go further if not enough pixels for subpixel-fitting
   if (xr - xl <= voisinage ||
   xl - voisinage< 0 || xr + voisinage>bounds.width) {
      leftBorder[y]  = xl - 0.5;
      rightBorder[y] = xr - 0.5;
      continue;
   }

   // now determine drop borders with sub-pixel precision
   leftBorder[y]  = fitStep(ip, xl, y, voisinage, false);
   rightBorder[y] = fitStep(ip, xr, y, voisinage, true);
} // end for y

if (leftBorder == null)
   return false;
else
   return true;
}
```

This method performs a line scan method to find the index where the drop falls
below the threshold. In this case, the drop has a low value compared to the
background. It starts by going in the left-to-right direction. As soon as it has found
that pixel, the variable xl will no longer increase and will be smaller than the width
of the bounds. This will activate the else if clause and will allocate the arrays for
the borders. The next step is to determine the index on the right-hand side using
the same methodology. However, now, the search goes in the right-to-left direction,
starting at the bounding box, and will determine xr.

The code mentioned in this method is generic Java code that is not specific for ImageJ2, but it performs the task in a similar way. It illustrates the fact that ImageJ2 plugins are not necessarily more complicated than or different from their legacy counterparts in terms of development. A difference between this plugin and a legacy plugin is the use of services such as the LogService interface. When the plugin is launched, it requests an instance of LogService using the @Parameter annotation:

```
@Parameter
private LogService log;
```

In the functional part of the plugin, this service is called to perform the logging of errors and other messages. An example can be found in the run() method of the plugin:

```
public void run() {
  HashMap<SHAPE_PARAM,Boolean> fitMe = tagParamsToFit();
  if ( ! fitMe.containsValue(Boolean.TRUE) ) {
    log.error("At least one parameter must be selected !");
    return;
  }
  //code skipped for brevity...
}
```

The log variable can be used to write messages to the log window. Based on the function used, they will be preceded by a label that indicates the type of the message. Methods such as error, warn, and info allow for different categories of messages to be reported.

Summary

In this chapter, we looked at the anatomy of plugins for ImageJ1.x and ImageJ2. We also looked at some of the specific constructs that are used in plugins for both frameworks. We examined how to compile, run, and debug our plugins using the tools provided by ImageJ or using the IDE. We looked at some established plugins and how they implemented plugins to perform a task in image processing.

This knowledge will be applied in the next chapter where we will create a plugin from scratch to perform image processing.

9
Creating ImageJ Plugins for Analysis

In this chapter, we will examine how to create plugins to perform analyses. This chapter will examine how to make a flexible plugin, and how to implement it in ImageJ to perform a simple analysis. The following topics will be dealt with in this chapter:

- Setting up a new plugin project
- Using a plugin to process and analyze images
- Adding user interaction and preferences
- Using external libraries
- Sharing your plugin

Plugin background and goal

In this section, I will briefly describe an image-processing problem that we will try to solve using a plugin. The problem is a general one that is encountered in many experiments involving living cells or organisms: they move and change shape. When we want to quantify certain aspects of the cells that we have imaged, we need to perform three basic steps:

1. Detect the object of interest.
2. Measure our object in the current frame.
3. Detect each object in our time series independently.

These steps are encountered in many different problems involving time series. For each of the three steps, we need to create a solution that solves the problem or quantifies the object in a meaningful manner. For detection, we can think of many methods that may be suitable to detect the object. When we think back to the topics discussed in *Chapter 4, Image Segmentation and Feature Extraction with ImageJ* we may think of a threshold-based technique to segment the image, and use a particle analyzer to find objects that contain specific features. For measurements, we can go back to *Chapter 5, Basic Measurements with ImageJ* where we looked at the basic methods to measure objects using ImageJ commands. The final component for this example uses the previous two methods for each of the identified objects.

To make our plugin more general and widely usable, we will also need to specify some parameters that will influence the outcome for each of these steps. The detection might need different criteria about what is a valid object depending on the data. To this end, we can create a generic dialog that will ask the user for input using a few input fields. I will give different examples of the same code that can be used in different scenarios.

Basic project setup

For this project, I will be using the Maven system to set up the project and the dependencies that are required. Most of the source code can also be run without these steps, but I will set it up using the NetBeans IDE using a Maven POM project. As we saw in *Chapter 7, Explanation of ImageJ Constructs* setting up a new project for ImageJ using Maven is done by navigating to **File | New Project**, and choosing **POM Project** from the **Maven** category in the wizard. For this plugin, I will use the project name `Object_Tracker`. After clicking **Finish**, the project will be created and should show up in the **Projects** view. If you cannot see the **Projects** view, go to **Window | Projects** from the menu to display it.

To start with, we need to tell Maven that we require ImageJ as a dependency. We do this by adding a `<dependencies>` section to our `pom.xml` file, as was shown in *Chapter 7, Explanation of ImageJ Constructs*. We will first look at how to create this plugin as a legacy plugin using all the standard coding of a legacy plugin. To code it as a legacy plugin, we will use ImageJ version **1.50b** as a dependency by adding the following code to our `pom.xml` file:

```
<repositories>
<repository>
  <id>imagej.public</id>
```

```
    <url>http://maven.imagej.net/content/groups/public</url>
    </repository>
  </repositories>

<dependencies>
<dependency>
    <groupId>net.imagej</groupId>
    <artifactId>ij</artifactId>
    <version>1.50b</version>
    </dependency>
  </dependencies>
```

The <repositories> section tells Maven where to find the sources for our dependencies, and in the optional <version> tag, we specify which version of ImageJ we wish to use. Note that if you start typing the version number in the tag, NetBeans will suggest version numbers that you can enter. At the time of writing **1.50b** was the latest version of ImageJ. If you leave this tag out, the version will be automatically set to the latest managed version. We will save the modifications to our POM file, which will trigger NetBeans to load the requested dependency from the repository and place it in the **Dependencies** folder within your project. If you issue the build command (**Run | Build Project**) for the project at this stage, we will still get an error. We are missing the source code for the plugin; this will be our next step.

To add our source code, we will need to add a new Java class file to our project. The following steps will let you create the main class file for this project; however, these steps are identical to generate other classes that you want to add to the same project:

1. Right-click on the Object_Tracker project and go to **New | Java Class…** from the context menu.

2. Enter Object_Tracker as the name for the new class, and set the **Location** to /src/main/java.

You will get a new java source file, and in the **Projects** view you will see the **Source Packages** directory is added to your project. You can now try and build the project again, which should now finish successfully. As a Maven project can also create Javadoc documentation for a project, we will also make sure that we add Javadoc comments to our class, and methods to document the API of our plugin. We will start the development of our plugin by implementing it as a PlugInFilter type.

Creating a basic PlugInFilter

To create a `PlugInFilter` implementation, we add the `implements` keyword behind the class name and specify `PlugInFilter` as the implementation. When you do this using an IDE, such as NetBeans, it will place a red squiggly underline under this statement. When you place the cursor on the line with the squiggly underline and press *Alt + Enter* (in NetBeans), the editor will give you a list of suggestions to rectify the mistake that we made. The first complaint is that NetBeans cannot find the `PlugInFilter` symbol because we haven't added it yet. Press *Alt + Enter* and select the option called **Add import** for `ij.plugin.filter.PlugInFilter`. You will now see that the import statement is added to your source file (usually at the top of the source file). We now still have a squiggly underline in our class statement as it is missing the overrides for the abstract setup and run methods. As explained in *Chapter 8, Anatomy of ImageJ Plugins* `PlugInFilter` requires these two methods to be present and overridden with your initialization code (setup) and your programming logic (run). Use the *Alt + Enter* method, and choose the option called **Implement all abstract methods** from the list of choices. At this stage, we have a basic `PlugInFilter` implementation that contains all the required elements.

Testing our current implementation

There is no functional code yet, but let's test what happens when we try to run the project at this stage. When you go to **Run | Run Project** from the menu, you will get a dialog that asks for the `main` class to be run. Since we did not specify a `main` method (yet), we cannot proceed and can only select cancel. We need to do two things: first, we need to add a `main` method to our source code file, and secondly, we need to tell Maven which class contains the `main` method. We will start with the first item on the list.

To add the `main()` method, we add the following code somewhere within the body of our class:

```
public static void main(String... args) {

}
```

This is a standard Java style declaration of a `main` method that takes a `String` list of parameters stored in the `args` variable. The triple dots behind the `String` type indicate that this method can be called with a variable number of `String` arguments ranging from none to many. This type of calling structure can be helpful if you want to run your plugin via a **Command Line Interface** (**CLI**). Since we will mostly ignore the input parameters for now, it is not important to use them within the body of the `main` method.

For the second step, we can modify our project in two separate ways. We can type the `<main-class>` tag in the `<properties>` tag in the POM file (see *Chapter 7, Explanation of ImageJ Constructs*), or we can use the features of the IDE. To edit how the project is run, you can right-click on the project in the **Projects** view and select **Properties** from the context menu. This will open the properties available for this type of project. Select the **Run** category from the left-hand side of the properties dialog:

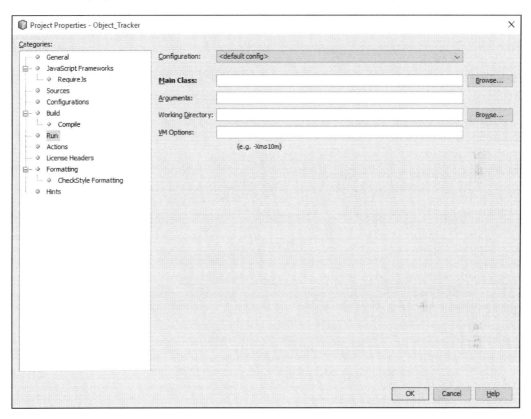

You can now see that there is an option to set the **Main Class**. By pressing the **Browse...** button, you are able to select the `Object_Tracker` class that contains our `main` method. You may also notice that you can specify **Arguments** to your `main` method. The content of this field will be used as input parameters to your main method's argument `args`. One option we might also want to enter at a later stage is the **VM Options** field. This option will allow us to control the amount of memory that is allocated to the application. For now, only select the `Object_Tracker` as the **Main Class**. This will generate two new files in NetBeans where the run configuration is stored: `nbactions.xml` and `nb-configuration.xml`. Alternatively, you can add the sections to the `pom.xml` file, as described in *Chapter 7, Explanation of ImageJ Constructs*.

Please note that using the **Properties** method, you will limit your application to the NetBeans framework. If you wish to exchange your code with others that do not use NetBeans, you always want to choose the pure Maven approach and define your `main` class in the `pom.xml` file directly.

If you try to run the project now by navigating to **Run | Run Project**, you will get no errors and the building will be successful. The only problem is that nothing happens; we don't see ImageJ, and our plugin cannot be found. We still need to implement our main method to make sure that ImageJ is launched. To do this, we add a new instance of ImageJ to our `main` method, and save the source file:

```
public static void main(String... args) {
  new ImageJ();
}
```

After fixing the error by adding the import for `ij.ImageJ`, we run our project and we will see the ImageJ interface. If you go to **Help | About ImageJ**, you will see that the version is indeed set to **1.50b**. However, when we look in the **Plugins** menu, we will not find our plugin there. We will use the same trick as shown in *Chapter 7, Explanation of ImageJ Constructs* to fix our plugins directory mix-up by adding the following code to our `main` method before calling `new ImageJ()`:

```
/* set the plugins.dir property to make the plugin appear in the
Plugins menu */
Class<?> clazz = Object_Tracker.class;
String url = clazz.getResource("/" + clazz.getName().replace('.',
    '/') + ".class").toString();
int lastIdx = url.lastIndexOf('/');

String pluginsDir = url.substring(5, lastIdx);
System.setProperty("plugins.dir", pluginsDir);
```

After saving the source file and running the project, we will now see our plugin in the **Plugins** menu. When you launch the plugin you will get an error specifying that this method is not implemented yet. This is caused by the fact that the body of the abstract `setup` and `run` methods only contain an exception that is being thrown (this depends on your installation of NetBeans and your templates). We have the plugin framework completed, and next, we will implement our functionality.

Implementing the setup method

We will start with implementing the `setup` method, which serves as a basic checkpoint to see if our plugin can process the currently active image. We can also use this method to make some preparations and perform some basic checks before we run our plugin. We will start with clearing the current statement from the body of the `setup` method and add a return value. The `setup` method requires that an integer value be returned, which tells ImageJ the type of image that can be processed using this plugin. We will also add some Javadoc comments to this function to explain what is going on in this function. For this project, I will assume that the following structure is the structure of the source code file:

```
//import section
import ij.ImageJ;

//class declaration
public class Object_Tracker implements PlugInFilter {
  //class-wide variables
  private ImagePlus imp;
  /*etc...*/

  //constructor
  public void Object_Tracker() {}

  //main method
  public static void main(String... args) {}

  //setup method
  public int setup(String arg, ImagePlus imp) {}

  //run method
  public void run(ImageProcessor ip) {}

  //additional methods follow below this point
  /*methods for image processing*/

}
```

You are of course free to deviate from this template (within the bounds of Java syntax and programming logic). This type of structure is common to Java files, and it contains some elements that are not strictly required, but which can be useful. The constructor is not required to be present in an ImageJ plugin. However, it can be useful to add it, as it allows an increase in usability when you want to call your plugin from within other projects. Using the constructor, you can implement certain initializations or assert control over how the plugin is created.

The return type and autocomplete

We will start with adding the return statement specifying the type of images that we expect to process. For this project, we are interested in quantifying objects over time in a single channel (for now), so we will expect to process stacks of either 8 or 16-bit. Therefore, we add the following return statement:

```
return DOES_8C+DOES_8G+DOES_16;
```

When typing in an IDE, you can use its autocomplete functionality to determine which type you wish to return. If you type DOES and press *Ctrl* + Spacebar you will get a list of the possible autocomplete options. You can use the mouse or the arrow keys to select an option from the list, and by double-clicking it or pressing enter, it will be inserted at the point you were typing. If the list of options is very long, you can also continue typing after you have pressed *Ctrl* + Spacebar. For every character that you add, the list will become more selective to match what you are typing. For example, when you type _1 after you typed DOES, you will only get the single option DOES_16. Another nice feature is that when you select an option from the autocomplete list, it will also show the Javadoc for that selection. However, you may have noticed that this didn't work here; the IDE stated that the Javadoc was not found. We will remedy this in the next section.

Javadoc for methods

As we saw, the Javadoc for our ImageJ project was not found. We will now fix this using the IDE, which only takes a few simple steps. First, we make sure that our Javadoc view is open by activating it. Go to **Window | IDE Tools | Javadoc Documentation** from the menu to activate the view. When we place our cursor on an object such as the DOES_16 statement that we entered above, the Javadoc view will display the same message that we noticed in the autocomplete window. However, it also displays an option at the bottom called **Attach Javadoc...** in the form of a link. When you click on it, a window will ask you for the location of the documentation. There is also a button called **Download**, which will automatically download the Javadoc for the ImageJ version that we listed as a dependency in our project. After clicking OK, you will now see that the Javadoc view shows the documentation for the DOES_16 field. You can also generate the Javadoc for your project by right-clicking on your project in the Projects view and selecting **Generate Javadoc** from the context menu.

We will now create our own Javadoc comments for our setup method. The easiest way to do this using the IDE is to place the cursor on the setup method and press *Alt + Enter*. An option will be displayed stating **Create missing Javadoc for setup**, which we will choose.

 You can also place your cursor above the method you wish to document, and type /**, and press *Enter*. In NetBeans, typing the start of a Javadoc comment and pressing *Enter* will autocomplete the Javadoc comment, and it will add the arguments and return type of your method as well.

After selecting this option, a Javadoc comment is added above the setup method containing the following information:

```
/**
 *
 * @param arg
 * @param ip
 * @return
 */
```

This is the standard content for a Javadoc section that describes a method with input parameters and a return value. Parameters are designated as @param followed by the variable name. There is one @param line for each parameter in the methods arguments list. To add information about the parameter, you can start typing right after the variable name (make sure that there is a space between the variable name and your description). The first line above the parameter list is meant to provide a brief description of the methods purpose. Let's add some of the information about the setup method:

```
/**
 * This is the setup method for the Object Tracker plugin
 *
 * @param arg input argument for control
 * @param ip Currently active image
 * @return DOES_8G, DOES_8C and DOES_16
 */
```

When you look at the Javadoc viewer now, you will see the text that you added is displayed and formatted. Please note that you can use standard HTML tags to format your text with paragraphs, headings, tables, and lists. At this stage it is possible to generate the Javadoc for your plugin and view it in a browser. To do so, right-click on your project in the **Projects** view and select **Generate Javadoc** from the context menu. After waiting a bit while the IDE is busy scanning the project and building the documentation, you can open the Javadoc in a browser by opening the `index.html` file from the `target/site/apidocs/` folder in the root of your project. Alternatively, you can click on the link in the **Output** view which can be activated by navigating to **Window | Output** from the menu. The result will be as follows:

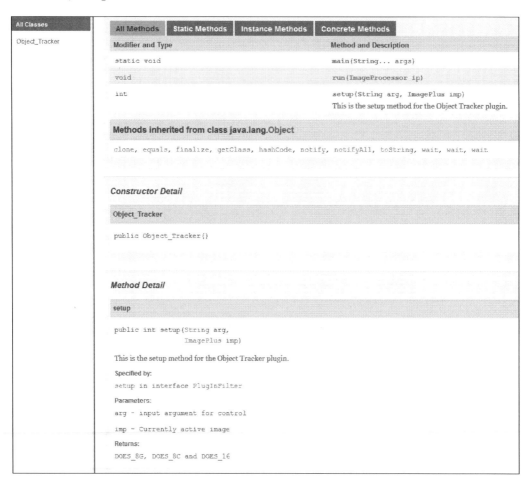

In the preceding screenshot, you can see the setup method with the text that we added as a description, and at the bottom, we see the details we entered for the parameters and the return value.

It is good practice to add this information as you develop your source code, both for your own benefit when you review your code weeks from now, as well as for other developers who may wish to use or expand your code for their own projects. As the Javadoc tool takes care of all the processing and layout of the documentation, you only need to add the descriptions for the methods and classes. I will not explicitly add the documentation sections in the code snippets in this chapter, but they will be part of the final source code. After this small digression, we will return to creating a plugin to detect objects.

Finishing the setup method

After completing the previous sections, we now have a setup method with a return value indicating that we will be processing all 8 or 16-bit images and stacks. We will now perform a few more checks that will be required for the processing to complete. The first step is to make sure that the ROI Manager is open so that we can see the detections and the results of our detection. At this stage, it might also be a good idea to think about the type of images we may want to process. Do we want to process RGB or multichannel images and stacks or only single channel stacks?

We will start with checking if the ROI Manager is available. To do this, we can use the getInstance() method from the RoiManager class. This method will return a value of null when it is not open yet; otherwise, it will return the reference of the ROI Manager instance. Add the following to the setup method before the return statement:

```
if(RoiManager.getInstance() == null) {
  new RoiManager();
}
```

If you used the autocomplete option to select the RoiManager class, NetBeans also automatically added the required import statement at the top of your source code file. If you copied and pasted the code, you will need to add the import statement yourself using either the *Alt + Enter* option or by typing it manually.

The only thing left to do in the setup is to check the image type; it needs to be a single channel image with a single frame or slice, or multiple frames and a single slice. The first step is to obtain the dimensions of the current image and then check whether it matches our specifications. For the current incarnation of the plugin, I will make these specifications binding so that when it fails, the plugin will not run. The code for retrieving the dimensions and checking whether they match our specifications is as follows:

```
//get the dimensions of the current image
int[] dims = ip.getDimensions();
if (dims[2] > 1){
  //more than 1 channel
  return DONE;
}
else if(dims[3] > 1 && dims[4] > 1) {
  //multiple slices AND frames
  return DONE;
}
```

The `getDimensions()` method returns a vector of length 5, with the width, height, channels, slices, and frames (in that order).

At this stage, I would like to introduce another useful feature of an IDE that will make your coding life much easier. When the IDE added the abstract methods for setup and run, it used the `ip` parameter name for both the `ImagePlus` type in the `setup` method and the `ImageProcessor` type in the `run` method. This is slightly confusing and inconsistent. The convention for `ImagePlus` objects is to use `imp` as a reference name, and `ip` for `ImageProcessor` references. We will now use the **Refactor** option in the IDE to fix this problem.

We will start by selecting the parameter that we would like to change; in this case, the `ip` parameter in the `setup` method. We then go to **Refactor | Rename** from the context menu or press *Ctrl + R*. You will now see that there is a red box around the parameter, and you can change the name by typing a new name. When you now type `imp`, you will see that only the names associated with the `setup` method are changed. This does not affect the parameter of the `run` method. Also, the Javadoc section is updated to reflect the new variable name. This is a great feature to use when changing the name of a variable, and it is much more effective than a search-and-replace style approach. If you would have used search and replace, the variable name in the run method may have also been changed, making it inconsistent again.

If we now run our project, we should see the plugin in the **Plugins** menu, but when we launch it, we will receive a `NullPointerException` exception. This is caused by the fact that we tried to retrieve the dimensions from a nonexistent image. So, we need to add a final check before we call the `getDimensions()` method to check if the `imp` parameter is not equal to `null`:

```
if (imp == null) { return DONE; }
```

This will make sure that nothing happens when you have no image open or the wrong kind of image compared to what the plugin expects. It is currently not very user-friendly. When the user activates a plugin, he or she would expect something to happen. It would be nice if there were some feedback to indicate why nothing happened. As an example, I will add a message stating that the plugin requires a stack to be opened before exiting. To do so, we add the following statement to the body of the statement checking for the image:

```
if (imp == null) {
   IJ.showMessage("We need a single channel stack to continue!");
   return DONE;
}
```

Now when you run your project and launch the plugin, the following message will be displayed:

This is much more user-friendly and avoids generating unnecessary errors, which can be confusing to users. Most of the errors and exceptions generated by compilers are cryptic at best, and most non-programmers will not understand what went wrong. Now that we have finished the setup method, we will now focus on implementing the actual functional code that will perform the processing.

Implementing the run method

As mentioned in *Chapter 8, Anatomy of ImageJ Plugins* the run method is the entry point for the `PlugInFilter` type. At this stage we know for sure that we have an 8 or 16-bit stack with a single channel; otherwise, we would have never reached the run method. We can now start implementing our algorithm to detect the object. After that, we will look at the required methods to measure the object in the current frame, and finally, how to process each object across frames in the case of multiple objects. We will start with the detection first, as this is the primary step that needs to be solved.

Detecting an object

To be able to detect an object, we need to know about some of the properties that make the object identifiable. This may sound simpler than it really is. The human visual system is highly capable of finding objects in all types of lighting conditions and situations. Computer algorithms are only starting to approach the same levels of detection that feel natural to humans. For this example, I will limit the detection of objects based on the intensity of the object relative to the background. I'm going to assume that the object we wish to detect is bright compared to the darker background, as is the case in fluorescence imaging for example. We will use the **Confocal Series** sample image to practice with as an example.

We need to make a few small preparations before we can start using this image. The image contains two channels, which is an exclusion criterion for our plugin! So we split the image into separate channels, and convert one of them to 16-bit before saving them both to disk as TIFF files. Using the knowledge from *Chapter 2, Basic Image Processing with ImageJ* and *Chapter 3, Advanced Image Processing with ImageJ* you should be capable of performing these steps. We will use a threshold to detect the object based on the intensity, and based on that threshold, create a selection that will be added to the ROI manager. For the detection, we will create a method called `performDetection()` that will be called from the `run` method. As we assume a stack, we will also need to add a loop to go over each of the slices. We will start with the loop statement in the `run` method:

```
int nFrames = imp.getImageStackSize();
for (int f=0; f<nFrames; f++) {
  imp.setSlice(f+1);
  ip = imp.getProcessor();
  performDetection(ip);
}
```

Notice the slightly odd behavior for the `setSlice` method. Unlike arrays and other indexed objects in Java, the slice indices for an image are not zero-based. This idiosyncrasy was observed back in *Chapter 2, Basic Image Processing with ImageJ*. Next, we create the method to perform the detection, and we add the following statements:

```
private void performDetection(ImageProcessor ip) {
    ip.setAutoThreshold(AutoThresholder.Method.Default, true);
    imp.setProcessor(ip);
    Roi roi = ThresholdToSelection.run(imp);
    rm.addRoi(roi);
}
```

This sets an automatic threshold using the default method (first parameter) and using a dark background (second parameter). When using the autocomplete option, many of these values will be filled in by default making it easier to write code, but not necessarily to understand it. We then add the new threshold to the current image using a reference to a class-wide variable that we added to our class definition (see the template for the class file that was mentioned earlier).

```
public class Object_Tracker implements PlugInFilter{
    private ImagePlus imp;
    private RoiManager rm;
```

This allows us access to the current image and the ROI Manager throughout our class. We also modify the setup method slightly to accommodate these changes using the `rm` reference to get the instance or store a new reference to the ROI Manager. We do the same for the class-wide `ImagePlus` variable (`this.imp`) by storing the current image that comes in with the `setup` method.

```
rm = RoiManager.getInstance();
if(rm == null) { rm = new RoiManager();}

this.imp = imp;
```

To add our thresholded object to the ROI manager, we use the `ThresholdToSelection` class (another `PlugInFilter` type) that comes with ImageJ. This is the class that is activated when you navigate to **Edit** | **Selection** | **Create Selection** from the ImageJ menu. This is a nice example of one plugin calling the `run` method of another plugin. This means that we can also use the `run` method of our plugin in other plugins or macros.

We will now test our plugin by running the project and opening one of the images we saved, before launching our plugin. It should now run through all the slices of the stack and populate the ROI manager at every frame. The ROIs look quite good, but there are still a few small problems. There are holes in some of the ROIs, and some ROIs have small isolated pixels that are not connected to the main object. In the next section, we will examine ways to refine the detection using the techniques that we learned back in *Chapter 4, Image Segmentation and Feature Extraction with ImageJ*.

Refining the detection

When we tested the plugin at the end of the previous section, we noted some shortcomings of the current detection method using only a threshold. We saw holes in the object and small isolated pixels that we would like to remove. This is something that can be achieved using binary processing as discussed in *Chapter 4, Image Segmentation and Feature Extraction with ImageJ*. We will now implement this processing before we convert the threshold to a selection. The first step is to take our ROI and use it to create a mask image, which we will process using the techniques that we learned in *Chapter 4, Image Segmentation and Feature Extraction with ImageJ*. To create our mask image, we do the following:

```
ImagePlus impMask = new ImagePlus("mask", new
  ByteProcessor(imp.getWidth(), imp.getHeight()));
impMask.setRoi(roi);

ImageProcessor ipMask = impMask.getProcessor();
ipMask.setColor(255);
ipMask.fill(impMask.getMask());
ipMask.invertLut();
```

This code is inserted between the `Roi roi...` statement and the `rm.addRoi(roi)` statement in the `performDetection` method. The first line creates a new image called mask with a `ByteProcessor` for the `ImageProcessor`; this results in an 8-bit image. The width and the height are set to be equal to the original image. This is important when you want to measure the object in the original image. If you create a mask directly from the image, its size will be the size of the bounding rectangle of the ROI. Next we add the ROI to the new image, and get a reference to the `ImageProcessor` for this image. This will allow us to modify the pixels of the mask. Next, we set the foreground color to white (255) and fill the mask with white. Finally, we invert the LUT for the binary processing. Next, we will perform the binary processing. We want to fill the holes and get rid of the isolated pixels.

We will start with filling the holes in the shape using the `Binary` plugin. This is a class that implements a `PlugInFilter`; however, the use is a little different this time. We first need to create an instance of the class, and then set up the class for our purpose. We will add the following code directly underneath the last statement of the previous code listing:

```
Binary B = new Binary();
B.setup("fill", impMask);
B.run(ipMask);
```

First, we create a new instance of the `Binary` class and add the import statement for `ij.plugin.filter.Binary` at the top of our source code file. Next, we set up the plugin to perform the task that we want, in this case, filling the holes in our mask. We do this by calling the `setup` method with a `String` argument (`"fill"`) and an `ImagePlus` argument (our mask image). Our own plugin has a similar form for the setup; this means that we could also choose to implement a similar system later on. In the last step, we call the `run` method of the `Binary` plugin, which will perform the actual processing on our image.

Next, we will use the erode and dilate operators to get rid of isolated pixels. We will run the erode operator three times and the dilate operator five times to create a smooth mask:

```
for (int i=0;i<3; i++) {ipMask.erode();}
for (int i=0;i<5; i++) {ipMask.dilate();}
```

These values are quite arbitrary and other values might be more suitable when using different images. Finally, we set a threshold on our mask image to obtain a new ROI using the `ThresholdToSelection` method, just like we did before:

```
roi = ThresholdToSelection.run(impMask);
impMask.setRoi(roi);
rm.addRoi(roi);
```

We use the `roi` variable again because we don't need the ROI that we created in the original image. We then add the new ROI to the ROI Manager, which is the last step for our detection. If you run the project and try it on the test images, you will see the effect of the binary processing—the ROIs are a bit more smooth and contain almost no isolated pixels anymore. The following image shows all the ROIs overlaid on the first frame of the original stack. I used the green channel for this example, but you can also try to run the plugin on the red channel.

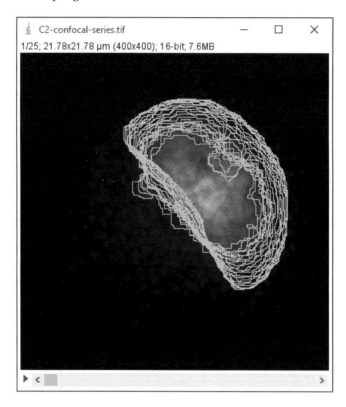

Detecting multiple objects

Up to this point, we assumed that we have only a single object in our frames. I will now look at a method that allows detecting multiple objects. To do this, we will use another technique that we learned in *Chapter 3, Advanced Image Processing with ImageJ*. There, we looked at Z-projections and how they can be used to flatten a stack into a single image. We will now use this same technique to define our search space to detect the objects in the time series. By creating a maximum intensity projection, we can visualize all the pixels that our object will occupy at one time or another during the time series. This projection will help us define the search space. For N number of objects that do not overlap, you will get N search spaces.

To start with, we need to create the maximum intensity projection. To do this, we can use the ZProjector class and set it to maximum intensity using MAX_METHOD:

```
//create a maximum intensity projection
ZProjector zp = new ZProjector(imp);
zp.setMethod(ZProjector.MAX_METHOD);
zp.doProjection();
ImagePlus impMax = zp.getProjection();

//set a threshold in the maximum intensity projection
ImageProcessor ipMax = impMax.getProcessor();
ipMax.setAutoThreshold(AutoThresholder.Method.Default, true);
impMax.setProcessor(ipMax);
```

We start by creating a new ZProjector instance using the original stack as an input. Next, we set the method to be used, and perform the projection. Finally, we retrieve the maximum intensity projection image using the getProjection() method. Next up, we will use the ParticleAnalyzer class to detect the objects in our maximum intensity projection that will define our search spaces.

To use the particle analyzer, we create an instance of the class and set its parameters to determine the search spaces. For this example, we want to find objects that are relatively large, so we will set a minimum size limit for the particles but not for the shape. To do this, we can use the following code:

```
//set the options for the particle analyzer
int nOpts = ParticleAnalyzer.ADD_TO_MANAGER;
int nMeasures = ParticleAnalyzer.SHOW_NONE;
double dMin = 500.0;
double dMax = Double.MAX_VALUE

//perform the particle analysis
ParticleAnalyzer pa = new ParticleAnalyzer(nOpts, nMeasures, new
ResultsTable(), dMin, dMax);
RoiManager rmMax = new RoiManager(true);
ParticleAnalyzer.setRoiManager(rmMax);
pa.analyze(impMax);

//get the detected particles
Roi[] searchSpaces = rmMax.getRoisAsArray();
```

We start by setting the options and the measurements that we want. In this case, we only care about the found objects' location, so we need ROIs at the end of the detection (indicated by the ADD_TO_MANAGER option). The option for measurements is set to none to avoid generating results or other objects (indicated by SHOW_NONE). We then initialize the particle analyzer using the options and sizes that we specified. Next, we create an instance of an ROI Manager that will not be displayed. This instance of our ROI Manager will be assigned to our particle analyzer before we analyze our image using the analyze() method. This is necessary because we don't want to measure these intermediate ROIs, we only use them to identify and process each search space. In the last step, we extract the search spaces as ROI objects from our temporary ROI Manager instance. With our search spaces defined, we can start the detections for each search space individually.

The detections can be created in a similar way as we saw before with a small alteration: instead of using the entire image, we want to perform our detection within the search space for the individual object. We can achieve this by setting the search space ROI on our image and duplicate it using the duplicate() method. We then have access to the pixels from this cropped region:

```
//perform the detection for each search space
for (Roi searchSpace : searchSpaces) {
  imp.setRoi(searchSpace);
  impProcess = imp.duplicate();
  for (int f = 0; f < nFrames; f++) {
    impProcess.setSlice(f + 1);
    ip = impProcess.getProcessor();
    performDetection(impProcess, ip);
  }
}
```

We do this for each of our search spaces using the for-each syntax, and perform the detection as before. There are some other alterations that are required to make this work, so take a look at the complete code listed in the code bundle at Packt Publishing's website.

Implementing the measurements

Now that we have our objects identified for each slice, we can start to look at measuring our object. We will use some of the knowledge from *Chapter 5, Basic Measurements with ImageJ* to design a measurement for this object. Depending on the type of object, we may want to look at different measurements that may be important, but I will start with some of the obvious ones for the type of ROIs that we created. Our ROIs are area selections, so the first metric that seems relevant is the area of the object(s). Other relevant measurements are the mean intensity and the shape of the object(s). We will implement the measurements in a separate method that we will add to our class. The method will have the following declaration:

```
private void performMeasurements() {
  Analyzer.setMeasurements(msrmnt);
  imp.unlock();
  rm.runCommand(imp,"Measure");
}
```

We will be using the ROIs in the ROI Manager so that we don't require an input argument. We will set the measurements according to the values that we discussed before by adding a variable called msrmnt at the beginning of our class declaration:

```
private static final int msrmnt = Measurements.SLICE + Measurements.
AREA + Measurements.CIRCULARITY + Measurements.MEAN;
```

This is used to set the measurements to the slice number, area, circularity, and mean. We use the `Analyzer` class and its `setMeasurements` method to get the desired results. Finally, we call the `unlock` method on our image to allow the macro command of the ROI Manager to gain access to our image for the measurements. If you omit this statement, the plugin will run without visible errors, but you will not get any results. To get the results, we call our measurement method directly after the loop has finished. In the next section, we will add some user interaction to our plugin, allowing us to change some of the parameters that are used in the detection. We will also introduce the preferences system of ImageJ to allow the storage of our parameters for future use.

Adding user interaction and preferences

The plugin that we have created thus far runs fine as a standalone plugin. However, it is also very easy to increase its power by allowing it to run in batch mode over a folder containing a large set of data files. This section will look at some of the changes that need to be incorporated for it to work. By setting certain steps as individual methods that can be called when the main class is instantiated, we can perform specific steps in a similar way as we have been doing for other classes. In our example, we used the `ParticleAnalyzer`, `ThresholdToSelection` and the `Binary` plugin classes in a similar way. The only requirements that we need to add are some constants and default settings that allow this class to work with minimal configuration. In the following sections, I will show you a few alterations that can make this class a bit more flexible to use in other plugins.

Settings and options dialog

We have several parameters in our plugin that will influence how it behaves. Variables, such as particle size and the thresholding method, will influence the outcome, and have to be adjusted to match the data. ImageJ allows you to set and get preferences that can be stored specifically for your plugin. It uses a key-value system that stores the value for a preference using a specific key name. The key name is a string, which must be unique to your plugin preferably. To set and get a preference, such as the minimum particle size, you can use the following syntax:

```
Prefs.set("object_tracker.minParticleSize", 500.0);
double DMIN = Prefs.getDouble("object_tracker.minParticleSize",
500.0);
Prefs.savePreferences();
```

The first line shows you how to store the double value `500.0` into a preference using the `object_tracker.minParticleSize` key. The naming of keys does not really have a strict convention, but using the `<class name>.<key name>` construction makes sure that the key will be unique and identifiable. The second line retrieves the setting from the preferences. The second value that is supplied is a default value. If the key does not exist, the `DMIN` variable will be set to this default value (in this case `500.0`). Finally, we can save the preferences using the `savePreferences()` method.

To change the values used in our plugin, we can display a small dialog that allows the user to enter values or make selections. When we use the dialog, we will save the results in the preferences. This means that we can run it as a batch process from this moment onward. To let the user set the key parameters for the detection, we can create the following preference dialog:

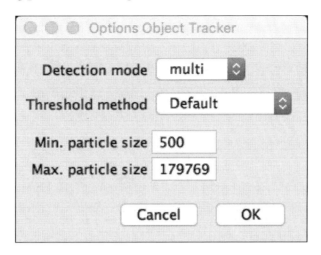

This is done using the `GenericDialog` class available in the `ij.gui` package. You start with creating an instance of the `GenericDialog` class, and then adding your fields of choice to it in the order that you wish for them to be displayed. For this example, we want to set the detection mode, the threshold method, the minimum particle size, and the maximum particle size. If you want, you could add more parameters to the preferences to allow more flexibility. The following code will create a dialog, add the fields, and display it:

```
//construct and show the options dialog
GenericDialog gd = new GenericDialog("Options Object Tracker");
gd.addChoice("Detection mode", (new String[]{"multi", "single"}),
DETECT_METHOD);
gd.addChoice("Threshold method", AutoThresholder.getMethods(), THRESH_
METHOD);
gd.addNumericField("Min. particle size", DMIN, 0);
gd.addNumericField("Max. particle size", DMAX, 0);
gd.showDialog();

//store the values
```

```
Prefs.set("object_tracker.detectMethod", gd.getNextChoice());
Prefs.set("object_tracker.threshMethod", gd.getNextChoice());
Prefs.set("object_tracker.minParticleSize", gd.getNextNumber());
Prefs.set("object_tracker.maxParticleSize", gd.getNextNumber());
```

At the end, we store the values that the user selected in the preferences using the keys. To obtain the values, we use the getNext<> methods. These are called in the order that the fields were added to the dialog, so the first call to getNextChoice will get the value from the first choice list (in this case the detection mode selection). The call to getNextNumber will retrieve the number from the first numeric field (in this case the minimum particle size). The order of the fields in a GenericDialog implementation becomes fixed when the fields are added, so this needs to be accounted for when retrieving the values. Refer to listing 9.2 for the complete code of the plugin.

Adding external libraries

When you have created a plugin for processing, you may want to add some functionality that is not available in the ImageJ core API. In this case, you may want to use an external library that has the functionality that you require. If you use Maven to set up your project, adding a library is as easy as listing it in your <dependencies> section of your POM file. As an example, I will show you how to add the Apache POI library to add an option to export the results of our work to an MS Excel file. The advantage of this library is that it can create an .xls(x) file on all platforms, regardless of whether MS Excel is installed. I will briefly show you how to create an Excel file, write some data to it, and then save the result as an .xls file.

Adding the dependency for Apache POI

To add the dependency of the POI project in your POM file, you will need to add the org.apache.poi project to your <dependencies> section. The IDE can help you with this process using its autocomplete feature. Let's suppose you create a basic dependency template similar to the one shown as follows:

```
<dependency>
  <groupId></groupId>
  <artifactId></artifactId>
  <version></version>
</dependency>
```

In this case, you can then place your cursor within the `<groupId>` tag and press *Ctrl + Spacebar*. You will then get a list of possible IDs that you can select. When you start typing the first part (`org.`), you will notice that the list becomes more limited as you continue to type. When you get to `org.apache.po`, the list only contains two options, including the POI package. If you repeat the process for the remaining tags, you may end up with the following dependency section:

```
<dependency>
  <groupId>org.apache.poi</groupId>
  <artifactId>poi</artifactId>
  <version>3.13</version>
</dependency>
```

At this point you can start to use the library and its interfaces, classes, and methods to create an Excel file (or Word documents and PowerPoint presentations). Please note that the packages for Excel files are designated with the **HSSF** moniker (**Horrible SpreadSheet Format**). After saving the POM file, you will get a new JAR file in your projects dependencies folder. In this, case it is the `poi-3.13.jar` file, and it contains the packages for the POI project. Make sure you build your project before proceeding further by navigating to **Run | Build Project** from the menu. We will now look at how to implement this library in the next section.

Creating an Excel file

To create an Excel file, we need to create a new instance of an Excel workbook using Apache POI. This is relatively simple using the `usermodel` package in `org.apache. poi.ss`. We create an instance of the Workbook interface and add a sheet with a specific name that will contain the data in a method we call `saveResultsToExcel`. Every time we add a new class, we can add our import statements automatically by pressing *Alt + Enter*. Just make sure that you select the correct ones. If you want to add the `Cell` class, you have multiple options, but we require the package for `org. apache.poi.ss.usermodel.Cell` in this example:

```
public void saveResultsToExcel(String xlFile, ResultsTable rt) {
  FileOutputStream xlOut;
  try { xlOut = new FileOutputStream(xlFile); }
  catch (FileNotFoundException ex) {
    Logger.getLogger(Object_Tracker.class.getName()).log(Level.SEVERE,
null, ex);
  }

  Workbook xlBook = new HSSFWorkbook();
  Sheet xlSheet = xlBook.createSheet("Results Object Tracker");
```

```
Row r = null;
Cell c = null;
CellStyle cs = xlBook.createCellStyle();
Font f = xlBook.createFont();
Font fb = xlBook.createFont();
DataFormat df = xlBook.createDataFormat();
f.setFontHeightInPoints((short) 12);
fb.setFontHeightInPoints((short) 12);
fb.setBoldweight(Font.BOLDWEIGHT_BOLD);
cs.setFont(f);
cs.setDataFormat(df.getFormat("#,##0.000"));
cb.setDataFormat(HSSFDataFormat.getBuiltinFormat("text"));
cb.setFont(fb);

int numRows = rt.size();
String[] colHeaders = rt.getHeadings();
int rownum = 0;
//create a header
r = xlSheet.createRow(rownum);
for (int cellnum=0; cellnum<colHeaders.length; cellnum++) {
  c = r.createCell(cellnum);
  c.setCellStyle(cb);
  c.setCellValue(colHeaders[cellnum]);
}
rownum++;

for (int row=0; row<numRows; row++) {
  r = xlSheet.createRow(rownum+row);
  int numCols = rt.getLastColumn() + 1;
  for (int cellnum=0; cellnum<numCols; cellnum++) {
    c = r.createCell(cellnum);
    c.setCellValue(rt.getValueAsDouble(cellnum, row));
  }
}
try { xlBook.write(xlOut); xlOut.close();}
catch (IOException ex) {
  Logger.getLogger(Object_Tracker.class.getName()).log(Level.SEVERE,
null, ex);
  }
}
```

In this example, I assumed that the data is in the form of an ImageJ `ResultsTable` object. In the loop, we go over the rows and then add cells to each row, one column at a time. We use the headers of the results table to make a header in the Excel file as well. We use a separate `Font` object (`fb` in this example) to make the style different from the data by making it bold. At the end, we save the results to a file using the generic `FileOutputStream` class.

To get the results table that is generated when you press the **Measure** button in the ROI manager, you can use the following code:

```
ResultsTable rt = ResultsTable.getResultsTable();
```

After asking the user for a file name, you can call the `saveResultsToExcel` method to generate an Excel file. The example code above works only to generate `.xls` files. To generate `.xlsx` files, you need to implement a workbook of the `XSSFWorkbook` class. The main difference between these two Excel formats is that the size of the data that can be contained on a sheet; `.xls` files have a limitation of 255 columns per sheet. If you expect to generate tables with more columns, you need to make sure to use the `XSSFWorkbook` class.

Sharing your plugin

When you have finished implementing all the routines and completed (extensive) testing, you are ready to distribute your plugin to the world. Currently, there are several options available to distribute your plugin, ranging from sending it using e-mail to an automated update mechanism in ImageJ. Here, I will discuss the latter option, which has some great benefits that makes it very user-friendly and efficient. Fiji, and ImageJ2 have a system that allows you to set a website as a source for your plugin. This website will be checked to see whether there is a newer version available, and if so, it will be automatically updated. The only thing your users have to do is add that site to their list of update sites to install and update your plugin(s). The following sections will describe how to setup this site, and how users can add the site to ImageJ (ImageJ2 and Fiji, specifically).

Creating a site

To create a site, you have different options available: you can host your own update site, or you can use the ImageJ Wiki site. I will now focus on the latter option as it is easy, free, and accessible to everyone. Note that your users need to have ImageJ2 or Fiji to be able to use this mechanism. For this section, I will assume that you are using Fiji, but it works in a similar manner in ImageJ2. To create the site, you can go to **Help | Update…** in the menu. In the window that opens, press the **Manage update sites** button on the bottom right to get the sites currently available.

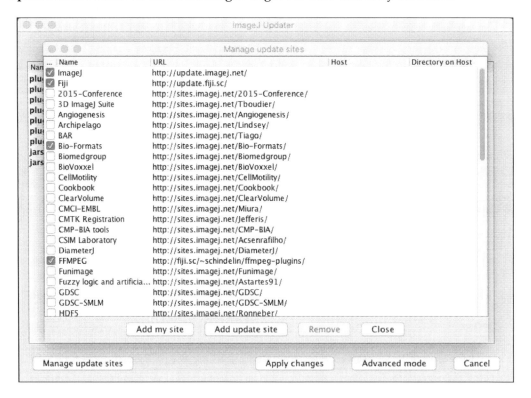

You can press the **Add my site** button in this window and either create a new account or use an existing account. If you already have an account, you only have to enter your user name, and if your password hasn't yet been stored, also enter your password. If you want to create a new account, you can enter a user name. If it doesn't yet exist, you can enter your e-mail address and press **OK**. You will receive an e-mail message on the account that you provided with a temporary password. You must then go to the Wiki login page at `http://imagej.net/Special:UserLogin` to change your password. Once you have modified your password, you can enter it in the **Add personal site** window of ImageJ. You are now ready to add your plugins to the website.

Uploading your plugin

To upload your plugin, you cannot just upload your file directly to the server. In order for it to be recognized as a proper update site and plugins, some additional files are required. Luckily, the ImageJ updater can also take care of this process for you. Open the updater by navigating to **Help | Update...** from the menu and click on the **Advanced mode** button. The first time you upload a plugin, you need to select the **View local-only files** from the **View options** drop-down list. You can now select your plugin on the left-hand side, and edit the details in the **Details** view on the right-hand side. By right-clicking on your plugin, you can open a context menu and select **Upload to My Site**. The **Status/Action** column should now display **Upload it**, and after pressing the **Apply changes** button and providing your credentials, the upload will start.

Summary

In this chapter, we developed a legacy plugin from scratch using the Maven system and the NetBeans IDE. We applied some of the image processing techniques that we learned in the previous chapters in our plugin. We saw how to add a basic user interface to our plugin, allowing the user to change some of the parameters that influence the way the plugin functions. We also saw how to store our settings in the preferences so that they can be recalled the next time we use the plugin. We added an external library to provide additional functionality that was not present in ImageJ. Finally, we looked at an automated way of publishing our plugin and sharing it with the world.

In the next chapter, we will look at the resources that are available to further your knowledge and skills in image processing and project development.

10
Where to Go from Here?

In this chapter, we will sum up the topics that were discussed and provide further resources that are available to continue developing your own plugins. The chapter will also look at some of the more advanced techniques that are available for developers. This chapter will cover the following topics:

- Basic development
- Additional tools
- Project management and feedback
- Other resources

Basic development

In this book, we have looked at many different ways of performing image processing and analysis. Automation using macros and plugins were introduced, allowing for infinite possibilities in processing and analysis. The topics in this book have been written for users who would like to start developing their own plugins and macros. Naturally, this book can only provide so much information within its pages, so this section is meant to provide some handles on how to proceed further along this path.

To start with, creating macros and plugins gets easier with repeated practice and learning from previous code (or other people's code). When creating macros, it is a good practice to make small macros that perform only a single step in processing. Then, by combining multiple macros, you can create a very versatile toolbox. Many useful tools in ImageJ, such as the ActionBar plugin, allow you to create a fast way to launch many different macros in succession. When developing in this fashion, make sure that you create macros that can be daisy-chained. The output of one macro can be used as input to the next macro and so on. This method will save you a lot of time, and it allows for almost any combination you wish to create.

For plugins, a similar advice holds. When you use a specific function many times over, it may be worth it to create a standalone class with helpful tools that you use often. By instantiating the class to gain access to its methods, you can reuse your code in many different projects. Some of the larger ImageJ projects use a specific tool class or classes. For instance, MtrackJ and NeuronJ both use a library of methods called `imagescience.jar`. When making plugins with an interface, it is also a good idea to build your actual processing or analysis routines in separate classes, which can easily be swapped when you develop new or better techniques.

There are many good resources available online to develop macros used in image processing and analysis. The most basic one is the repository on the ImageJ website, which contains many excellent macros that perform basic and more advanced tasks and can be found at `http://imagej.nih.gov/ij/macros/`. Another good resource is the Fiji website, which contains a lot of information about image processing and analysis described in a cookbook (`http://imagej.net/Cookbook`). This cookbook is based on the defunct MBF microscopy resources and explains how to process and analyze specific images using the tools supplied with Fiji.

Some very good resources have been published as well. *Digital Image Processing* by *Burger and Burge* is a comprehensive textbook that focuses on the algorithms used by ImageJ functions. This provides a mathematical background to some of the processing functions in ImageJ as well as image transformations and interpolations. Examples in their work are based on or extracted from ImageJ source code. Another good resource is Gonzalez and Woods' *Digital Image Processing*, which uses MATLAB for image-processing examples. It, however, also provides a mathematical background as well as techniques such as fuzzy logic in image processing. Many of the examples used can be translated to ImageJ as an exercise. A good source for algorithms is the *Numerical recipes* book series, which was written in the C/C++ language. Many of the algorithms can be translated into Java without too much hassle. Another resource that can help in understanding the physics of image formation, as well as the basics of signal processing, is *The Scientist and Engineer's Guide to Digital Signal Processing* by Steven Smith (available on `http://www.dspguide.com/`).

Finally, if you wish to develop plugins that utilize a user interface, it is a good idea to look at many different plugins with interfaces. In *Chapter 8, Anatomy of ImageJ Plugins* we looked at different examples of plugins with a basic and advanced interface. Some of these examples have a very clear and intuitive interface that can be used with minimal documentation. There are many good publications on good designs of interfaces as well as online resources that can show you examples of good and bad designs. Examples of published books include *Universal Principles of Design*, which examines common concepts in design based on experience and psychological knowledge. Another good resource is the book *Don't make me think, revisited*, which is written with web design in mind. However, the core principles are the same for desktop applications and ImageJ plugins.

Another good online resource is the blog of Joel Spolsky, a developer involved with Microsoft Excel, at `http://www.joelonsoftware.com/uibook/chapters/fog0000000057.html`. Although the examples mentioned are slightly historic, the general truth behind the observations still holds true. It also has a lot of useful insights into designing and running projects.

To learn more about plugin development in the new ImageJ2 framework, there is good documentation and background available on the Fiji website on the framework (`http://fiji.sc/ImageJ2`) and some of the library functions such as ImgLib2 (`http://fiji.sc/ImgLib2`). There is also a good collection of example projects available to test and discover how to use these concepts, for instance, how to work with images using ImgLib2 (`http://fiji.sc/ImgLib2_Examples`). A set of ImageJ tutorials is available on GitHub as well. They can be cloned using your favorite Git implementation from `https://GitHub.com/imagej/imagej-tutorials/`. As ImageJ2 is still under active development and currently is at release candidate status, many changes will still be implemented before it is released as a final version.

Additional tools

Many of the examples described in this book can be designed and built using the built-in editors of ImageJ and Fiji, but if you want to develop more advanced plugins, setting up an IDE would make you work faster. As a learning tool, an IDE might not be the best option. The learning curve of the IDE itself can be steep, and also, it can make you lazy. IDEs can be quite clever and analyze your code to provide automatic importing of classes, implementing the required methods, and variable checking and casting. These tools are handy, but it is important to understand what is happening when the IDE suggests these options. Of course, the spellchecking and completion of variable names makes sure that you will make fewer typos, but you should never blindly rely on it. The analysis of code can be quite sophisticated, but it cannot predict what the developer has in mind. This can sometimes result in very odd behavior or errors that may be hard to debug.

To work with an IDE such as NetBeans, as described in the previous chapters, many resources are available from the developers of the software. Tutorials for NetBeans can be found at `https://netbeans.org/kb/index.html`, which contains tutorials, examples, and videos to use the IDE to develop projects. Packt Publishing also has books about NetBeans IDE usage, specifically *NetBeans IDE 8 cookbook* and *Mastering NetBeans*.

Besides investing time in an IDE, it is also helpful to invest time in understanding and learning how to use a revision system, such as Git. The workflow when using a revision system is a little different than when just developing code directly. A revision system would only work if you commit your changes on a regular basis and provide useful commit messages. If you are the only developer on a project, you would not run into many problems such as difficult code mergers and conflicts, so the process becomes relatively straightforward. With the help of a graphical frontend for Git, the whole process becomes manageable and accessible, even for beginners.

Make sure you are comfortable with using Git before you start a multideveloper project. Conflicts and mergers can get complicated and resolving them may become hard if binary files are involved. Many IDEs have a revision system built in (many times, it's under the **Team** menu, that is, in Eclipse and NetBeans). Whether you use the built-in system or a standalone interface, there are a few good resources to look at before using them. They will help in understanding what the system is capable of (and what not). A very good resource is the *Git Book*, which can be downloaded from `https://git-scm.com/book/en/v2`, while printed copies are also available. *Chapter 2*, *Basic Image Processing with ImageJ* and *Chapter 3*, *Advanced Image Processing with ImageJ* give a clear overview of how to use Git in daily life. It mostly uses the command-line interface for the examples. However, the graphical frontends that are available use the same terminology. Packt Publishing has practical books for working with Git as well, including *Git Version Control cookbook* and *Git: Version Control for Everyone*, which contain practical examples and use cases for development.

For Subversion, another revision software package, a similar online resource is available at `http://svnbook.red-bean.com/en/1.7/index.html`. It details the basis of subversion and explains the process of committing changes and the revision process. This resource also assumes a mostly command-line approach to dealing with the repository system, but the terminology is similar to most graphical frontends. Most clients that are compatible with Git also support Subversion, and there are packages available that can convert a Subversion repository into a Git repository without (too much) loss of the structure of the repository. One graphical frontend that I use on a regular basis is SmartGit/Hg by Syntevo. It runs on all platforms and has support for GitHub repositories. It is free for non-commercial work, but requires a license when used for commercial projects.

Project management and feedback

There are a few difficulties that come with working with a team on a project. Such work requires an additional layer on top of the actual development. For this, there are project-management solutions available that can organize projects. These solutions usually contain multiple levels and are usually built on top or on part of a revision system. Most project-management solutions contain (at least) issue trackers and road maps. Most of these solutions are mostly built as administrative tools and do not directly interface with the developed code (at least in the case of ImageJ plugins). They, however, allow for developers to keep track of progress and plan future development and for end users to provide feedback and indicate where bugs and errors exist. Most of these solutions run on a server that can be approached via a browser, and they support multiple users as well as unregistered guest users.

Different solutions exist, and the choice for a solution should be based on your needs and equipment available. Server hosting nowadays is not really complicated or expensive, so the choices are quite broad. Some options are available are GitHub. They can host projects, provided they are open source, for free. Other options are hosting your own solution, such as Redmine. Redmine is an open source project management solution written in the Ruby language. Other open source examples are Launchpad, used by many Canonical projects related to Ubuntu and Trac used by NASA's JPL and for Tor development. Besides bug trackers, they also have some form of time management and road map. They also allow us to host files and documentation. Redmine also supports news and forum pages for projects, as well as user management on a project basis.

If you wish to develop code in a more managed setting, these tools may be useful to investigate. Many of these systems can work on a small network or even just on your local computer. To use any of these systems in a more accessible setting, you require a computer system with a revision system installed, such as Git or Subversion, and a functional and configured webserver application, such as Apache, Nginx, or Tomcat. For Redmine, a Ruby, and a *SQL database installation is also required. Some systems also require a PHP installation for certain functionality. Although this may sound complicated, many of these functionalities come standard with a **LAMP** (**Linux, Apache, MySQL, PHP**) server distribution, such as the Ubuntu Server edition. Many server-hosting companies provide a fully configured LAMP server without additional management. Also, many of these project-management suites come with simple installers that are configurable for many different use cases.

Using the software is done via a basic login page, which allows different users with different levels of access to the management system. Privileges can be granted to allow certain users to create, modify, and manage projects. Other users can be added as reporters. They can access most parts of the management systems, such as the trackers and the forum pages, but not the settings of the project. In the case of Redmine, most of the pages are based on a Wiki-like syntax for the content, allowing rich and feature-rich documentation with graphics and other layout options. Most issue trackers have room for different categories, such as bugs, features, or support. This allows us to make classifications of the type of issue that is being reported as well as their priority. Issues can also be assigned to specific developers, making the division of labor for multiple developers clear and easy.

Resources and documentation for Redmine is available online at `http://www.redmine.org/projects/redmine/wiki/Guide`, which uses Redmine itself and functions as a clear example of the workflow. A published book called *Mastering Redmine* is available as well.

Other resources

When developing code, it can be useful to check whether certain solutions to your problem already exist. When a good implementation already exists and is used, it saves you time in developing a library or functions. For example, many good solutions to generate Excel files exist in the form of libraries written in Java. One such example is the Apache POI project, which allows for the reading and writing of Excel files (and other Microsoft Office products). Implementations of this library exist for many software packages as well as other Java-based software. For instance, the xlwrite wrapper function developed for Matlab by Alec de Zegher uses the Apache POI project to create Excel files (`http://www.mathworks.com/matlabcentral/fileexchange/38591`). It should not to be confused with the `.xlswrite` wrapper function supplied by MATLAB, which uses ActiveX to write Excel files, thereby requiring a Windows platform.

For resources that you wish to use as libraries, you can use Maven, as described in *Chapter 7, Explanation of ImageJ Constructs*. Maven is part of most IDE installations (either as part of the core or as a separate plugin). By including the libraries as dependencies in the `<dependencies>` tag of the POM model, they will automatically be added to your projects' dependencies list. Additional resources on how to use Maven in a project can be found on the Apache Maven website (`https://maven.apache.org/guides/index.html`), which is the main developer of the Maven system. There are also some books and videos available to set up and develop software using Maven, for instance, *Apache Maven 3.0 cookbook* and *Maven: The definitive guide*.

Summary

In this chapter, we looked at some of the steps that can be taken after finishing this book. I focused on some tools that are available to make the development of software more organized and professional. Some resources for each of these components were included, both ones available online as well as published works.

Index

O

OME-XML (Open Microscopy Environment-XML) project **5**
Open… button **124**

P

particle analysis
preparations 96-98
preprocessing 96-98
semiquantitative colocalization 95
PlugInFilter
creating 162, 192
current implementation, testing 192-194
measurements, implementing 209
setup method, implementing 195
PlugInFrame type 163
Plugin Javadoc 147
plugins
about 135
anatomy 161
background 189, 190
Coloc2 181, 182
ColorTransformer2 175, 177
compiling 167, 168
debugging 167-171
examples 171
framework 129, 130
goal 189, 190
Goutte_pendante 183-188
ImageJ main class 135, 136
ImagePlus class 136
ImageProcessor class 137
in Fiji 172
in ImageJ 172
legacy plugins 162
MtrackJ 177-181
MultipleKymograph 173-175
options dialog 210, 211, 212
preferences, adding 210
project setup 190, 191
Roi class 138
RoiManager class 137
settings dialog 210-212
sharing 215
site, creating 216

running 167
SciJava plugins, compiling 168
uploading 217
user interaction, adding 210
WindowManager class 136
Wiki login page, URL 216
PlugIn type 162
Point ROI 74
point selections 79
Poisson process 30
POM file 150, 151

R

regions
about 74
area selections 74
line selections 74
Regions Of Interest (ROIs)
about 74
class 138
Manager 74
RoiManager class 137, 138
run method, PlugInFilter
detection, refining 204, 205
implementing 202
multiple objects, detecting 206-208
object, detecting 202-204

S

saveAs command 108
SciFIO 5
SciJava plugins
@Plugin annotation 165
about 164
commands 166
compiling 168
services 166
segmentation 49
selections
area selections 75
line selections 79
point selections 79
sequences
loading 22, 23

setup method, PlugInFilter
  auto-complete 196
  finishing 199-201
  Javadoc, for methods 196-199
  return type 196
Shot noise
  correcting 30
signal processing
  URL 220
signal-to-noise ratio (SNR) 30
stack 18
stack processing
  about 40
  maximum projection 41-43
  projections 41
  time series data, normalizing 46-48
  time series data, processing 46-48
  time series, processing 46
  volume, rendering 43-46
  volume, viewing 43-46
  Z stacks, processing 40
Subversion
  URL 223
syntax highlighting 103

T

Tagged Image File Format (TIFF) 3
time series
  about 20
  data, normalizing 46-48
  processing 46
  uneven illumination 33-35
  viewing 28
tools 222, 223

U

user input, macro
  about 106
  choices, adding 109, 111
  image, saving to folder 107-109
  input check, performing 112-115
  specific file, opening 106

V

volumes 20
Volume Viewer 44

W

WindowManager class 136

Z

Z stack
  about 18
  images 20
  processing 40

Thank you for buying
Image Processing with ImageJ
Second Edition

About Packt Publishing

Packt, pronounced 'packed', published its first book, *Mastering phpMyAdmin for Effective MySQL Management*, in April 2004, and subsequently continued to specialize in publishing highly focused books on specific technologies and solutions.

Our books and publications share the experiences of your fellow IT professionals in adapting and customizing today's systems, applications, and frameworks. Our solution-based books give you the knowledge and power to customize the software and technologies you're using to get the job done. Packt books are more specific and less general than the IT books you have seen in the past. Our unique business model allows us to bring you more focused information, giving you more of what you need to know, and less of what you don't.

Packt is a modern yet unique publishing company that focuses on producing quality, cutting-edge books for communities of developers, administrators, and newbies alike. For more information, please visit our website at www.packtpub.com.

About Packt Open Source

In 2010, Packt launched two new brands, Packt Open Source and Packt Enterprise, in order to continue its focus on specialization. This book is part of the Packt Open Source brand, home to books published on software built around open source licenses, and offering information to anybody from advanced developers to budding web designers. The Open Source brand also runs Packt's Open Source Royalty Scheme, by which Packt gives a royalty to each open source project about whose software a book is sold.

Writing for Packt

We welcome all inquiries from people who are interested in authoring. Book proposals should be sent to author@packtpub.com. If your book idea is still at an early stage and you would like to discuss it first before writing a formal book proposal, then please contact us; one of our commissioning editors will get in touch with you.

We're not just looking for published authors; if you have strong technical skills but no writing experience, our experienced editors can help you develop a writing career, or simply get some additional reward for your expertise.

OpenCV Computer Vision with Python

ISBN: 978-1-78216-392-3   Paperback: 122 pages

Learn to capture videos, manipulate images, and track objects with Python using the OpenCV Library

1. Set up OpenCV, its Python bindings, and optional Kinect drivers on Windows, Mac or Ubuntu.

2. Create an application that tracks and manipulates faces.

3. Identify face regions using normal color images and depth images.

OpenCV 2 Computer Vision Application Programming Cookbook

ISBN: 978-1-84951-324-1   Paperback: 304 pages

Over 50 recipes to master this library of programming functions for real-time computer vision

1. Teaches you how to program computer vision applications in C++ using the different features of the OpenCV library.

2. Demonstrates the important structures and functions of OpenCV in detail with complete working examples.

3. Describes fundamental concepts in computer vision and image processing.

Please check **www.PacktPub.com** for information on our titles

Printed in Great Britain
by Amazon